HOCKEY
BY GERALD ESKENAZI

GROSSET & DUNLAP
A National General Company
Publishers • New York

cop. 2

Library of Congress Catalog Card Number: 73-826

ISBN: 0-448-11531-4 (Trade Edition)
ISBN: 0-448-03933-8 (Library Edition)

For Ellen,
My Little Princess

Contents

CHAPTER I
The Story of Hockey

A black puck skimming across the milky-white ice, a grunt and a thud, a windup unleashing a powerful slap shot, a frenzied crowd lustily cheering a goal—these are some of the ingredients that make up the topsy-turvy world of ice hockey. It is a game that unites a country such as Canada; and a game that plays to standing-room-only in the United States, where most of the spectators have never even laced on a pair of skates.

It is a special sort of world, with its own tradition, terminology, heroes and villains, all of it inseparable from the fans, who are tied into the action because of their proximity to the ice and to one another. Hockey fans themselves will admit to being the most loyal, the most vocal, the most demanding, and the most excitable of sports fans.

Yet the game as we know it has existed for only a relatively short time. It has been in its major-league form in the United States for less than fifty years, and was virtually unknown in Canada before the turn of the century. Europeans, who probably originated the game and who are now among its strongest adherents, waited more than two thousand years before organizing it and establishing uniform rules.

Just how old is hockey? Fairly old. Archaeologists have unearthed Greek ruins that include friezes showing men attempting to hit a ball with a curved stick. Was it hockey? Not as we know it. And the game wasn't played on ice. But it was a game based on the same idea: to hit the ball before the opposing player did.

Since the earliest times, men have played games with sticks and ball-like objects. Sometimes the contest was for personal triumph; often, it was for the glory of a city or country. Naturally, it was easier to play during the summer, spring and fall than in the winter, since winters were too severe for any existing sport. Roads were difficult for travel, and ice skates were unknown. The only smooth, flat areas available for sport were the frozen lakes, ponds and rivers, and how could a game be played as the participants slipped and slid?

In sixteenth century Europe, a game in which dozens of people took part was played for a town's honor, with as many as thirty people on each side. The object was to chase a ball and knock it over a line. Such games, often wildly humorous, often dangerous, but never slow, were the forerunners of field hockey, a sport immensely popular in western Europe. Often enough, the players' sticks hit the opposition's shins —perhaps leading to the name "shinny," which the game came to be called. Even today, ice hockey among unorganized players is known as shinny.

The word "hockey" most likely was derived from the stick the players used. It was curved at the end, hooked just like a shepherd's crook, which, in French, was called *hoquet*.

Fun has always been inherent in sports, and it is perhaps in the spirit of fun that another theory has been put forth regarding the origin of the word hockey: that it derived from the Mohawk Indian word *hoghee,* meaning "it hurts." The Indians, too, played field games with balls and sticks, but in their version the losers were whacked over the head.

In any event, it is the Dutch who are credited with putting players on the ice. The first serviceable ice skates appeared in Holland about 1860. The skate was a metal blade, and the player merely strapped one onto each of his shoes. Soon, thousands of British troops sent to Canada took with them not only one of their favorite games, field hockey, but also the British version of these first blades. Unaccustomed to long, frozen winters, the soldiers put the "skates" to good use. They took to the ice in an attempt to keep themselves occupied. And as they moved on to new encampments, they soon took their skates—and a new game they had begun to play on the frozen ponds—across Canada. It was field hockey on ice—a new version of shinny. The game was formless, with as many as fifteen players to a side, and it had ill-defined rules.

As the strange new game spread across Canada, more people became interested in it. Teams were formed at colleges, army camps and social clubs. It was soon apparent that a uniform set of rules was needed.

Many cities in eastern Canada lay claim to "originating" hockey. Certainly, it had mushroomed there by the 1870's, with many teams and leagues battling. But experts generally agree that the first game played according to specified rules was probably staged in December, 1879, at Montreal. In that French-speaking city,

student teams from McGill University played—with thirty skaters to a side. The influence of field hockey was strong, but the students soon gave this new game a character of its own. They lowered the number of players on a team to nine. Still, the sport bore little resemblance to today's version.

Spectators attending a professional hockey game today are accustomed to watching the contest from seats within a warm building, despite the presence of ice only a few feet away. There is adequate light to observe the action. The players are well-insulated against the cold from the ice, and their padding protects them as well from impact, the thrusts of opponents' sticks and elbows, and the flying puck. They are also protected from excitable spectators by four-foot-high partitions that surround the rink, as well as the ushers and security police. The ice is usually uniformly smooth, even when air temperature gets a bit warm. But in the early days at McGill University, and at other rinks, it was a very different situation.

The game was played, first of all, on natural ice. That meant there were treacherous ridges and soft spots on the surface. Uniforms? A team sweater was worn over a shirt, which was tucked into a pair of pants. The players were in full view of the spectators, with a wooden barrier, perhaps a foot high, separating them. When fans didn't approve of something a player did, it was an easy shot to hit him with a potato. Many of the games were played without a goal cage. Often, two poles were dug into the ice behind a goalie, and if the puck passed between the poles a goal was scored. The puck barely deserved the name—it might have been a tin can, or a pine knot, or a scrap of rounded rubber. But innovations evolved rapidly from growing numbers of players. Baseball, already popular in Canada, suggested ideas for protection. Instead of using magazines

Typical London scene in 1890's: Young men on way home from their jobs gleefully take part in pick-up game, as depicted in London Illustrated News.

under their shirts to deaden the impact of a puck, goalies substituted a catcher's chest protector. Magazines were used to protect shoulders, and if a player sheared Eaton's mail-order catalog in half, he had a practicable pair of shin guards, strapped on by strips of rubber cut from the inner tube of a tire. A stick could be purchased for a quarter, and if youngsters didn't have the money to buy one, they could always "make do" with a branch from an elm tree. Even the name "rink" was borrowed from another sport. For centuries, a rink (a Scottish word meaning a course) was a place where the Scottish game of curling was played.

Despite all such makeshift devices, within six years of the game at McGill the new sport was already vying with lacrosse as the Number One pastime of Canadians. Hockey sticks were being manufactured in Montreal and other major cities, skates that could be clamped on were in use, and there was a boom in the hockey equipment industry. This intense interest led, in 1885, to a major meeting in Montreal among hockey followers. Out of that meeting came the Amateur Hockey Association of Canada—the first organized hockey association. In that same year, the first league was formed in Kingston, Ontario. The league wasn't ambitious. It had only four teams: Queens University, the Royal Military College, the Kingstons, and the Athletics. They played under new AHA rules, the most significant of which reduced the number of players on a side from nine to seven. The reduction enabled individual players to show their skills more dramatically, and the sport was given impetus by the ruling, the association and the league.

The major problem facing would-be players, though, was still a place to play. Natural ice had its well-known hazards. It was not always convenient to find a frozen body of water. Because fans and players displayed such keen interest, cities soon began building arenas around natural ice surfaces. For the first time, the sport moved indoors. A new problem arose—lighting. Oil lamps were dim, and cast shadows. It was difficult at times for players and spectators to see the puck. But it was an improvement on the outdoors, and the sport prospered as Canadians faced the new century.

Hockey still had a long way to go. A recurrent problem was the goal—no feasible cage had been invented as yet. But a man whose name was lost to history got an inspiration one day while walking near the docks, as he observed fishermen mending their nets. He bought some of the netting, attached it to a pair of poles, and thus contrived the goal cage. Now the spectators and referee would be able to see when the puck went into the net.

Other leagues began forming, but the AHA remained the strongest. Although soldiers had taken the game with them across the country, the sport was little known in the west. It needed a jolt, something to put it on page one, to make the entire country aware of it.

The jolt came in 1892, in the form of the Stanley Cup. It was donated by the Canadian governor general, Frederick Arthur, Lord Stanley of Preston, who had been impressed with this purely Canadian game. He directed that the Cup be given annually, starting in 1893, to the top team in Canada, which would be determined by a playoff. Of course, Lord Stanley had no inkling that the Cup would eventually go to professionals, or that it would become, for Canada, a symbol of glory that rivals the World Series pennant in baseball. The beautiful silver cup cost ten pounds ($48.67). Today, it costs more than that merely to engrave the names of the winning team's players on its base.

The lure of the Stanley Cup and the na-

Montreal A.A.A., 1889 Eastern champions. Back row (from left): A. A. (Archie) Hodgson, left wing; W. L. Maltby, president; J. A. (Jimmy) Stewart, point; W. (Billy) Barlow, spare, and A. E. (Archie) McNaughton, center. Front row: W. S. (Bunny) Lowe, right wing; T. L. (Tommy) Paton, goal-keeper; Allan Cameron, cover point, and J. A. (Jack) Findlay, rover. (Hockey Hall of Fame)

Lord Stanley, donor of Stanley Cup, symbol of world pro hockey supremacy.

(Hockey Hall of Fame)

Montreal Hockey Club of 1893, first team to win the Stanley Cup.

(Hockey Hall of Fame)

(Public Archives of Canada)

Ottawa Hockey Club players who captured the Stanley Cup in 1905.

tional recognition it meant led to the formation of many rival leagues to the AHA. Dissension finally led to the breakup of the AHA in 1899, whereupon a splinter group, the Canadian Amateur Hockey League, came into being. Why it insisted upon the term "amateur" is a mystery. The better clubs were hardly that. But it was considered bad form to accept money for playing, and Canadian leagues were adamant about retaining their amateur standing. So it fell to the United States to field the first acknowledged professional hockey team in the world.

The fans in the United States were not so concerned with the concept of amateurism as were their brothers across the border, who had been steeped in traditional British thinking when it came to sports. In 1903, a dentist from the midwest, J. L. Gibson, formed a team in Houghton, Michigan, and gave it the grand name of Portage Lakes. He imported Canadian "amateurs" to Houghton, a copper-mining town, and paid them to play. In that respect, hockey has changed little over the years— virtually all professional players in the United States still are Canadian. Dr. Gibson took his team on barnstorming tours throughout the United States, to towns whose top players were no match for the visitors. How could the towns compete? Simple. They began importing players, too! In 1904, the International Pro Hockey League was formed, composed of United States teams with Canadian players.

Portage Lakes remained the best team. In twenty-six games in the new league it scored the remarkable total of 237 goals, winning twenty-four times and losing only twice. Finally, a Canadian team in Sault Ste. Marie, Ontario, concluding that "if you can't beat 'em, join 'em," did just that. It became the first club north of the border to acknowledge itself as professional.

Gibson, meanwhile, continued to lure some of Canada's top players. They included Edouard Charles ("Newsy") Lalonde, a sensational lacrosse player who was voted, in a 1950 poll, Canada's top athlete for the first half of the twentieth century. Fred ("Cyclone") Taylor and Hod Stuart also turned pro. The three, who ultimately were elected to the Hockey Hall of Fame, each received up to $500 a game.

Many Canadians nonetheless still "looked the other way" in recognizing professionalism. It wasn't unusual for a Canadian "amateur" to play a few games in Dr. Gibson's league, take the money, and return home to play for an amateur team. But because Dr. Gibson's league paid its players so handsomely, it soon became necessary for the amateur teams to search for ways to cut down expenses. A simple solution was devised: reduce the number of players. The number of men on a team was shaved from seven to six, a figure that has remained constant.

The prospect of money and prestige also led a club called the Dawson City Klondikers, from the heart of the Yukon, to challenge Canada's dominant club, the Ottawa Silver Seven, for the Cup. It resulted in one of the most bizarre quests in sports history. The challenge was made during the winter of 1904, and Ottawa accepted. Now the Klondikers had to raise the money to travel the four thousand miles to play.

The Klondike was a haven for a motley assortment of people—thieves hiding from the law, gold prospectors, miners, dance-hall girls, investors, bankers, men who had come to the Yukon in search of adventure and wealth. Since the hockey players on the team didn't have the necessary fare for the trip, they sought a backer, and found one in Colonel Joe Boyle, a man who had struck it rich. He financed the trip for $3,000. The trip was to be a long and tortuous one, involving travel by dog sled, bicycle, stagecoach, boat and train.

It was 20 degrees below zero as the men undertook their mush to Skagway, which was 350 miles from Dawson City. Bands played, children waved banners, and young girls threw kisses. To a resounding command of "Mush!" the dogs pulling the sleds took off, followed by the trotting hockey players, who waved back to the crowd. That first festive day the Klondikers traveled 46 miles. They moved an additional 41 miles the second day. But by the third day, signs of frostbite became apparent as blisters appeared on the feet of several players. They could go only 36 miles on the third day. The players' feet were so seriously affected that the men had to remove their boots, wrapping their feet in socks and cloth and newspapers.

Somehow, they managed to reach Skagway—a port city which was their only way out—but much later than they had originally hoped. The boat that was to transport them to Seattle, the next major stop on their trip, departed only every five days. When they arrived in Skagway, they found they had missed the boat by two hours. Close to the point of exhaustion, suffering from assorted injuries, the players greeted the delay with mixed emotions. They had only until January 13 to reach Ottawa. Now there were five days to rest, but there was also a possibility of missing the game.

Even after their ordeal, the players were concerned about keeping in shape. They found a rink in Skagway that measured 40 by 50 feet (matchbook-size compared to their standard rinks, which were about 200 feet long and 80 feet wide) and held a practice exercise while they waited for the next boat. But half the rink was covered with sand, and it dulled the skates. They decided against further training on such a surface.

At last their boat arrived, a coal scow that offered hardly any comfort. But it was their only possible transportation for the 900-mile trip to Seattle, Washington, from which point they had to backtrack another 200 miles to get to Vancouver. At last, they boarded a train for the long cross-country trip. There were no training facilities available, of course, but they were able to use the smoking car for workouts. It was small, and there wasn't enough room to accommodate all the players at once, so the players went into the car in shifts and did rope-skipping exercises.

On January 12, 1905, the day before the series was scheduled to start, the Klondikers arrived in Ottawa. They tried to have the opening game postponed. The contest was to be a best-of-three series, with only a few days between games. But the Ottawa team refused to shift the first game to a later day, and after their long trip the visitors bedded down at the noisy Russell Hotel.

They played as might be expected the next night. Ottawa trounced the visitors, 9-2. If there was one favorable aspect of the Klondikers' play, it was that they had held Ottawa's Frank McGee, considered the finest player in the game, to only one goal. Although it was obvious they couldn't beat Ottawa on the ice, at least one Klondiker talked up a good game afterward. "Who's this guy, McGee?" he asked disparagingly. He was to find out three days later, in the second game of the series. McGee scored 14 goals—a figure no professional hockey player before or since has achieved—and the Silver Seven demolished the gang from the Yukon, 23-2. The headlong trip from Dawson City for the Klondikers had been in vain—nearly a month of hardship endured for two quick defeats. But at least they made a bit of money, thanks to Colonel Boyle.

The amateur clubs in Canada were losing money, however, and in 1908, Canada formed the Ontario Professional Hockey League. That same year the first European hockey group, the International Ice Hockey Federation, was also formed.

Sprague Cleghorn of Renfrew.

Fred (Cyclone) Taylor.

The original member nations of the international group were Great Britain, Bohemia, Switzerland, France, and Belgium. The players in these countries, however, were dedicated amateurs—and have remained so since. In fact, Canada is probably the only nation in the world that has produced a significant number of professional players. Although Czechs, Swedes, and Russians have always been included among the world's finest players, they are "amateurs."

The formation of Canada's professional league quickly heightened interest in ice hockey in that country, which had grown to accept the "play-for-pay" boys. Colorful players with equally colorful names soon became national heroes: Minnie McGiffin,

Spunk Sparrow, Sprague Cleghorn and Billy Coutu commanded attention that previously had been reserved only for lacrosse players. In 1910, the National Hockey Association was formed. It was later to become the powerful National Hockey League associated today with the best in professional hockey. The NHA began with only five teams—Renfrew, Haileybury, Cobalt, the Wanderers and the Montreal Canadiens. The Canadiens are still here, the oldest professional hockey team.

The NHA was prospering, and the players demanded more money—demands similar to those that would shake the hockey world in 1972. Art Ross, who would become a member of ice hockey's Hall of Fame, was the game's top defenseman, playing for Haileybury. He threatened to form a rival league unless he would be paid more money. Ross became angered and made his threats when the team's owner wanted a ceiling of $6,000 for the whole team's salary. Ross himself had been earning $2,700. Eventually he was persuaded to stay, and in later years had many outstanding seasons with the Wanderers before moving into management.

Other people besides Ross considered forming rival leagues. There was a major problem, however: where to play. Only eight artificial-ice rinks existed in 1911, and not one was in Canada. That didn't deter the Patrick family—Joseph, the father, and Lester and Frank, the sons—from proceeding with an outrageous plan to form a hockey league on Canada's west coast. If rinks weren't available, they'd build their own, using artificial ice. All they needed were players. So the Patricks, a daring and innovative family, went to work. First, they took a poll in Victoria, British Columbia, to find out how many people were interested in joining them in their venture. They found one man—and he was willing to purchase only $500 worth of stock in their bizarre scheme. Undaunted, they did it on their own, forging ahead with plans for a 10,500-seat arena in Vancouver, British Columbia, that was to be the world's largest indoor arena. They also broke ground on a 3,500-seat arena in Victoria. Then they formed the Pacific Coast Hockey Association, with Victoria, Vancouver, and New Westminster as members.

The NHA didn't look kindly upon these proceedings. A mixture of envy and fear greeted the Patricks' announcement that they were scouting for players. Most good players were in the east, the home of the NHA, competing for positions on NHA teams. But the NHA, which wanted to have its cake and eat it, too, had overlooked something when its teams signed the good players. Most of the players had only one-year contracts, if they had contracts at all. And it wasn't unusual at that time for a mere handshake to serve as a binder.

There was little loyalty, then, to teams. Even among the NHA clubs, it wasn't unusual for good players to flit from team to team, winding up where the compensation was highest. In this spirit of competitiveness, the determined Patricks, armed with money, stormed east. Without compunction, they offered some players double their current salary to move west. They found out which contracts were expiring, and which had been sealed with a handshake, and acted accordingly. In an incredibly short time, the Patricks not only formed a rival league, but had two new rinks for their players!

The first Pacific Coast Hockey Association game also turned out to be the first game in Canada ever played on artificial ice. It was held on January 2, 1912, with 3,500 fans on hand at Victoria. One observer noted: "With all due deference to cricket, we think hockey is a trifle faster." Three nights later, 10,000 people turned out at Vancouver for that rink's debut.

Suddenly the West Coast discovered ice hockey. The new league quickly surpassed the NHA in interest. Although only a few years old, the NHA was reluctant to introduce new rules to improve the game, and the owners squabbled among themselves. Frank Patrick, however, was a man of ideas. His innovations account for many elements of ice hockey as played today. Even so obvious a suggestion as having players wear numbers on their backs originated with Frank Patrick. At that time it enabled many of the new fans out west who were unfamiliar with the players to identify them. By thus acquainting the fans with the players, the wily entrepreneur was also able to sell programs.

Ottawa Hockey Club, champions of the National Hockey Association, 1914–15. Third row (from left): Cosy Dolan, manager; Jack Darragh, forward; Art Ross, defense; Horace Merrill, defense; Frank Shaughnessy, manager. Second row: Angus Duford, forward; Sammy Herbert, goal; Alf Smith, coach; Clint Benedict, goal; Leith Graham, forward. First row: Eddie Gerard, forward, and Captain "Punch" Broadbent, forward.

Cy Denneny of Ottawa.

The players in the new league were performing so well that the Patricks impudently asked the NHA if it would care to send its own championship team out west for a World Series of Canada. The proposal did not amuse the NHA owners, who were still smarting from the player raids. They flatly refused. The Patricks, free to go their own way, continued to improvise modifications of the rules. Now a goaltender was permitted to leap or dive for a shot, instead of merely standing his ground. This new freedom imbued goalies with a new personality, and the game gained another dimension. The trend also encouraged a netminder to devise a trick or two. Some goalies busied themselves loosening a goalpost's anchor while the teams clashed at the other end of the rink. When the action came close and it was too much to take, a goalie would simply knock the top of the goalpost loose with his arm—and stop play.

The Patricks stood firm on two phases of the game, however: they played seven-man hockey, and they kept the goal judge stationed directly behind a goal, rather than positioning him in a booth in the stands. A goal judge on the ice had to withstand not only the physical impact of the club's best shots without flinching, but the jeers and insults of fans, as well. One judge from Victoria, John V. Johnson, often recalled a game in which a fan behind him repeatedly screamed, "You're blind, Johnson!" Johnson didn't appear to notice the continual abuse. But on one shot that headed directly at him, Johnson ducked. The puck landed in the stands and caught the fan squarely on the head. Johnson looked around and inquired, "Who's blind now?"

In the league's second year, the NHA reluctantly agreed to send its champion players to face the rival league's best for the Stanley Cup. Victoria won, but the NHA refused to part with the coveted trophy.

During one of the games, 15 offside infractions were called in the first five minutes. Fans hooted the constant play stoppage. In those days, a player was offside if he was ahead of the puck-carrier when receiving a pass. So for the next season, the PCHA adopted a new rule, one that accelerated the action of the game even more. The Patricks painted two blue lines across the width of the ice, dividing the playing area into three equal parts. They permitted forward passing in the center zone. The game was now opened up so dramatically that forward passing was soon allowed in all three zones.

The playoff was another Patrick innovation. Although many fans today are convinced that playoffs were instituted by owners merely to gain additional money after the end of the official season, that is not the reason they began. The Patricks sensed that there was something unfair if a team lost a key player through injury, and had to suffer through the season without him. Also, some clubs simply took more time to get moving, and weren't able to overcome a huge early lead by an opponent. The brothers instituted the playoff, having the runner-up play the first-place club for the post-season championship.

It was obvious to the Patricks that fans liked to talk about the game. In particular, the Patricks noted that baseball fans discussed baseball long after the season had ended, especially statistics, such as the number of home runs, or hits, or errors, that players had made during the season. In ice hockey, the goal-scorer alone earned a point. If a man didn't get a goal, there wasn't much information alongside his name. The player setting up a goal merited recognition, too. The Patricks gave him credit for an assist, and even carried the assist concept a step farther. They decided to award two assists, the second one going to the man who gave the puck to the player who gave it to the goal-scorer. As long as no opponent touched the puck during the passing, the two players handling the puck just prior to a goal each received an assist worth one point.

Unlike its West Coast cousin, the NHA was not dominated by an influential family. Intramural warfare was the rule, and teams dropped in and out of the league with startling frequency. Managements shifted, players were unhappy over salary, teams changed names. Then World War I changed the face of the NHA even more. At least 25 of the league's top stars enlisted in the Canadian armed forces. One battalion attracted so many NHA stars that it applied for an NHA franchise—and was granted one for the 1916-1917 season. That was the last season for the NHA. The great Cy Denneny of Toronto was the figurehead in a situation that almost led to a players' strike. Denneny had moved to Ottawa and had told his club that he preferred to play in his new home town, since his family was there. Denneny was suspended when he refused to play for Toronto. After two months, Denneny was still under suspension, and players spoke of forming a union. The other NHA owners pleaded with the Toronto management to free Denneny. Toronto finally did, in exchange for a goalie and $750—a record deal at the time. But everything seemed to be against the NHA. A nationwide scandal erupted when it was discovered that the armed forces team in the league had recruited players with no intention of sending them overseas for combat. After half a season, the battalion was ordered transferred to Europe, but that move then required a change in the standings. The season was divided in half, with the first-half leader competing with the second-half winner for the championship. It was the first playoff in NHA history.

The Canadiens won the playoffs, defeating Ottawa, and prepared to play the PCHA champion for the Stanley Cup. Excitement of Cup play usually makes itself felt throughout Canada, but this time emotions were mixed because the PCHA champion was Seattle—a United States team. Heretofore, Canadian teams had vied for the Cup exclusively. If Seattle now won, the Cup would have to cross the border—a nightmare never imagined by Lord Stanley! Seattle demanded assurance that if its team triumphed, the NHA would relinquish the Cup. The NHA reluctantly agreed. Seattle won—and so, for the first time, the Cup left Canada. It was a bizarre ending to a strange season, and it also ended an era.

On November 26, 1917, the National Hockey League was formed. It remains today perhaps the strongest league in the sports world, with virtually all of its teams playing to capacity audiences. Its beginnings were hardly prestigious. Actually, the league evolved because the NHA wanted to rid itself of a troublesome owner, Eddie Livingstone of Toronto, and the only way to oust him was to form another league that excluded Livingstone's club. Major Frank Robinson, the NHA's president, became so indignant at this subterfuge that he refused the presidency of the "new" league. Frank Calder, the NHA secretary, was then appointed president—a post he held until his death in 1943.

The original member teams of the new league were the Canadiens, Toronto, Ottawa and the Montreal Wanderers. The Wanderers (Montreal's "English" team), one of the really outstanding teams, had many fine players and great traditions, but they only lasted a little over a year in the reorganized NHL. Their building burned down, and without a place the play, they withdrew from the league. Meanwhile, the Patricks were beginning to feel a financial pinch. Their big arenas drew large crowds

Boris Mikhailov (13) of Soviet Union scores in first period against Team Canada and Russians went on to win fourth game, 5–3, at Vancouver.

Valery Ivanovich Vasiliev (6) back-checks Canadian player and gets puck in front of Soviet goal.

during the hockey season, but there weren't enough events during the rest of the year to draw fans to help pay the mortgage. Today's hockey teams play in buildings that are adaptable to other activities for most of the year, but in the early days there was little besides hockey to attract people. Another league was formed out west by the Western Canada Hockey League—consisting of Calgary, Regina, Edmonton, and Saskatoon. The new league made playoff arrangements with the Patricks' league, and for a time there was renewed interest and good attendance. But the Patricks' difficulties continued, nevertheless. In 1923, Seattle was eliminated, and the two western leagues merged, sharing arenas to reduce expenses.

It was merely a holding action. The NHL was already considering expanding to the United States and taking in the big Eastern cities where money was plentiful. More gate receipts meant more money for the players, and the western league could not hope to acquire star players if it couldn't pay as much as the NHL did.

From all their investments, Frank and Lester Patrick were netting only $3,000 a year apiece. The NHL had to do something —fast. In February, 1924, it startled Canada by announcing that a Boston team had been granted a franchise in the NHL for the following season, with more United States teams slated to join as soon as possible. And to encourage attendance of the English-speaking population of Montreal, a franchise was also granted to a club called the Maroons. The Canadiens, composed exclusively of French-Canadian players, had failed to attract the non-French citizens of Montreal, who also wanted representation.

The 1924-1925 season saw the first United States team, the Boston Bruins, make its debut. As in the past, though, what began as a bright season for the NHL ended in confusion. Hamilton (Ontario) wound up first in the league—but the players refused to enter the playoffs unless they received more money, contending that when they had signed their original contracts the full season was for only 24 games, whereas now it was 30. Calder refused to listen to the players' demands. He barred them from the playoffs and the right to compete for the Stanley Cup. Instead, he ruled that the league champion would be the winner of a series between the second-place Canadiens and the third-place Ottawa team.

Although the league didn't realize it, it was on its way toward stability, as well as toward a different outlook. Henceforth, the United States would play a major role in the NHL. The league accepted two more United States teams for the 1925-1926 season—the New York Americans and the Pittsburgh Yellow Jackets. Pittsburgh, which had been a member of an amateur league, changed its name to the Pirates, trading on the nickname of the baseball club. The Hamilton situation deteriorated; the team was under suspension. Finally, Hamilton was dropped from the league, and its players were signed by the New York team.

Perhaps the first radical change in North American ice hockey took place the following year. 1926 was the year in which the structure of the game changed, and the NHL emerged strong and united. Indeed, its transformation was so major that it was another 40 years before any such drastic change took place again. In 1926, three more United States teams joined the NHL: the New York Rangers, Chicago, and Detroit. With the Montreal Canadiens, Toronto and the Boston Bruins, they were to form the backbone of the league. Before the new teams joined, the western league had finally called it quits. The Patricks couldn't meet the high salaries demanded by their players, who wanted what NHL skaters were receiving. The Patricks, forced out of business, sold their league to the NHL for $250,000.

The move thus enabled the Patricks to withdraw with some money, and the three new clubs were able to draw from a large pool of talent to stock their teams. Other clubs in the NHL were also able to acquire players from out west. The Boston Bruins probably came off best—they gained Eddie Shore from Edmonton.

Shore's legend came with him, and in future years one could never be sure whether all the stories he told were fact or fiction. This much we know: he had a difficult time growing up on the prairies of western Canada. His father, a farmer, often thrashed the boy when he failed at jobs that even a grown man wouldn't tackle. Shore not only did his share of the harvesting, but performed minor surgical operations on cows, horses and pigs. Young Shore grew into a lean, determined man who knew only one way to play hockey— the hard way. He became a defenseman at a time when hockey defensemen were supposed to lay back, away from the offensive action. But he soon shattered the pattern. He was extremely fast and tough, and startled fans and players with devastating rushes that traveled the length of the rink, bringing him eyeball-to-eyeball with the opposition's goalie. If anyone got in his way, he would swerve with amazing speed, or knock the player down. It usually didn't seem to matter much to him which alternative was taken.

The Rangers also fared well in acquiring western players such as Frank Boucher and Bill and Bun Cook, a trio that would form the nucleus of many powerful teams.

When the 1926-1927 season began, the NHL consisted of ten clubs, divided into two divisions: the Canadian Division and the American Division. The Ottawa Senators, the Maroons, the Americans, and the Pirates eventually dropped out over the next 15 years, but the remaining teams were there to stay. They gave the league the continuity it had been lacking. That same season the Stanley Cup became the property of the NHL. Amateurs would no longer compete for the Cup—only NHL clubs could. The Cup gave prestige to the league, as well as a strong identity.

For almost 50 years it was generally recognized that the Stanley Cup winner was the world's best team. To most people that also meant that the National Hockey League was composed of the world's best players.

In the 1950's the Russians began getting serious about the game and, in fact, dominated it on an international, amateur level. They were considered amateurs, even by their own standards. Few people in North America ever believed that the Russians could possibly give any sort of battle to the top pros.

Curiosity was more the response to the news early in 1972 that the Russians had challenged Canada to field its best players for an eight-game series—four in Canada, four in Moscow. Almost every expert predicted an eight-game sweep for the Canadians in the September series. Things, however, didn't go right from the beginning. There was the problem of who would play. At first, this didn't seem much of a problem at all. The best players in the National League were Canadian—every last one of them—so it would simply be a matter of choosing the top ones. The WHA, however, had spirited away Bobby Hull, Derek Sanderson, Gerry Cheevers and J. C. Tremblay, among others. Since the National League had been asked by Hockey Canada to form the squad, the NHL wasn't about to put what it considered traitors on the squad, even though the "traitors" were Canadians.

The club that played the Russians was called Team Canada, and was chosen by Harry Sinden, once the leader of the Boston Bruins.

"We've got nothing to gain in this series," said Sinden. "If we win, everyone will say we were supposed to, that we were the pros. And if we lose, the same people will say we weren't all we were cracked up to be."

As the games approached, doubts began to nag the Canadians. The games would be staged in two parts—the first four in Canada in early September, the next four in the Soviet Union later in the month. But the opening week of September is NHL training-camp time. Players never report to camp before then. Yet, to be ready for the Russians, the Canadians would have to report a month earlier. Many of the players didn't want to. They had off-season jobs and felt that if they started playing hockey in August, they would be exhausted by the end of the regular season the following April. A compromise was reached. The players would report in mid-August. That gave them only two and a half weeks.

By the time the series began in Montreal, the games had built to a crescendo of excitement. To the Canadians, the Russians were a profound mystery. "That's the thing about them," said Brad Park of the Rangers. "We don't really know what to expect." Scouts had seen the Russians work out. The goaltending looked bad, the skaters seemed small, the defense appeared awkward, and the forwards didn't have hard shots. Why had they asked for these games if they were so deficient?

Canada soon found out. The Russians beat the National Hockey League in the first game. The Russians, it turned out, had been practicing for months, and had permitted the scouts to see, as one player explained it, "exactly what they wanted us to see." The Russians confounded the Canadians with their stamina and stick-handling ability. They never let up, passing in the same fashion whether they were ahead or behind. Also, the goalie, Vladislav Tretiak, had practiced stopping the puck by having a device similar to a cannon explode pucks at him at 130 miles an hour —20 miles an hour faster than anyone on Team Canada could shoot.

The series became a crusade. Could the Canadians come back? They won the second game at Toronto, then tied the third at Winnipeg. But they lost the fourth Canadian game at Vancouver and the crowd booed.

"We'll still win this," said Phil Esposito of the Bruins, who had become the team leader. Esposito, playing without the injured Bobby Orr, surprised many fans with the way he took charge and a superb display of moves that hadn't been demonstrated even during the season of his 76 record goals.

The Russians won the first game in Moscow. But Canada took the series as Paul Henderson scored on a pass from Esposito in the closing seconds of the final game.

No Stanley Cup victory ever meant more to the league. The implications of this series were profound. The National Hockey League had found a country that could give it a legitimate battle. No sooner were the games ended than the league and the Russians discussed further competition, and perhaps even a series between the Stanley Cup champions and the Russians.

CHAPTER II

The Dropouts

Pittsburgh Pirates

Although the Pirates adopted a proud old baseball name, they never seemed to attract many fans. They had some "name" players from time to time—such as Lionel Conacher, Roy Worters, and Harold Cotton—but as a team the Pirates had the saddest record of any club in the young, energetic league.

The squad was owned eventually by Big Bill Dwyer, the bootlegger who also owned the New York Americans. In a desperation move, Dwyer appointed Benny Leonard, a former world's lightweight boxing champion, as the club's president, and in 1930 the team was moved to Philadelphia. Leonard was president in name only, and the situation in the City of Brotherly Love, coach Cooper Smeaton recalled, "was terrible."

"Benny thought he'd knock Philly dead," said Smeaton. "The first day we got there we had a meeting with all the newspaper people. We offered each of the writers $25 a week to keep our name in the paper. If the club made a go of it, they'd get more. They laughed at us. They wanted $50 a week."

A compromise settlement was reached, but many of the spectators didn't know the first thing about hockey. Each day Smeaton would dash off three hundred words on a typewriter, have them mimeographed, and distribute the story to the newspapers.

As the season progressed, problems mounted. Bills weren't being paid. Smeaton had to finance four trips himself. He was nearly stranded with his team at the railroad station when a check presented for the club's fare to Chicago bounced. He tried unsuccessfully to reach Leonard, but he finally reached Dwyer's lawyer by telephone in New York, and the funds arrived shortly before the train was scheduled to leave.

Other than Cooper Smeaton, who eventually became a trustee of the Stanley Cup, there were few bright spots in the team's history. The club had started its first season with Odie Cleghorne (one of the first to try the concept of quick line changes) as player-coach. Six years later few of the original Pirates remained, and the team (known in its final year as the Quakers) dropped out of the league in 1931.

Ottawa Senators

The Senators started as a professional team in 1907. They captured four Cups and four first-place finishes before they moved to St. Louis in 1934 and dropped out in 1935.

The early clubs were powerhouses, and included such stars as Fred ("Cyclone") Taylor, Martin ("Marty") Walsh and Percy LeSueur, the goalie. Players in the early 1900's often scored five or more goals in

Andy Aitkenhead of
Rangers protects
goal against
Senators in 1934
game at Madison
Square Garden.

Frank (King) Clancy,
defenseman for
Senators in 1926.

a game. LeSueur, who played seven seasons, until 1913, was among the foremost goalie every year—although his average was about 5.5. He eventually made the roster of hockey's Hall of Fame, and played for two Ottawa Cup champions, in 1909 and 1911. The Senators won their last Cup and last regular-season title in 1926-1927.

Taylor was a marvel in a career that saw him reach success first in Eastern Canada and later in the Patricks' Western League. He played rover and center. Often he was even too fast for his teammates. In his first game with Ottawa he was put on a line with Alf Smith and Harry Westwick, two older players, and they just couldn't keep up with him. He was shuffled back to defense, where he starred for two years. His cyclonic rushes from one end of the ice-covered rink to the other helped propel him to legendary status, and gained him his nickname. He was even reported to have scored a goal while skating backward. Taylor, who earned the Order of the British Empire for his service during World War II, played only two seasons with Ottawa and was transferred to Renfrew in 1910. From there he migrated westward and, at age 30, started a new career that lasted nine more seasons.

Walsh led the NHA scorers three times. He was noted for his one-game scoring outbursts. During Ottawa's 1911 Stanley Cup victory over Port Arthur, he scored ten goals; seven goals went in against Montreal in 1908; six each against Galt in 1910 and Renfrew in 1911; and twice he scored five goals in a game. During Walsh's five seasons with Ottawa, the Senators won two Cups.

Other potential Hall of Famers found their way to Ottawa: Cy Denneny, Frank ("King") Clancy, Harry ("Punch") Broadbent, and Frank Nighbor. Clancy played his first season on the Senators'

Cup-winning team of 1922. He was traded in 1930 when Conn Smythe, owner of the Maple Leafs, paid a record $35,000 for him. Broadbent led the league's goal-scorers in the 1921-1922 campaign with 32 goals in 24 games. Some say the Lady Byng Trophy was invented for Nighbor. After winning the most-valuable-player award in 1923, he captured the Lady Byng for three straight years.

Success didn't help Ottawa at the gate, however. The club played in a civil-service town, meaning there wasn't much extra money around. It dropped out of the league in 1931 in an attempt to assess where it was going. It resumed play in 1932, but lasted only until 1934. The franchise was shifted in 1935 to St. Louis, where the team was known as the Eagles, but consisted mostly of the Ottawa players. After one season in St. Louis, the club disbanded.

Montreal Maroons

The Maroons were formed in 1924 to help keep the new Forum Arena busy, at the urging of Montreal's English-speaking community. They lasted until 1938, finishing first once and winning two Cups. James Strachan and Senator Donat Raymond, the operators of the Forum, bought the franchise for $15,000. For their first season, 1924-1925, they brought in Clint Benedict as goaltender and Punch Broadbent for scoring, both from Ottawa. The manager was Cecil Hart, who had resigned as a Canadiens' executive. Benedict was in on four Cup wins—three with Ottawa, one with the Maroons—and his average in Cup play was an outstanding 1.35 goals a game. In playoff appearances he turned in ten shutouts.

The Maroons finished fifth in the six-team league for their first season. They started out their second season with two

Rangers and Maroons meet in '34 Stanley Cup playoffs at Madison Square Garden.

new, important faces—Nelson ("Nels") Stewart and Oliver ("Babe") Siebert. Stewart, Seibert, and Stewart's boyhood friend, Reginald ("Hooley") Smith, who was elected to the Hockey Hall of Fame in 1972, formed the Maroon's "S" Line. Stewart, known as Old Poison, played with the club for seven years and became the first player to score 300 goals in a National Hockey League career. In his rookie season Stewart led the Maroons to a second-place finish when he topped the scorers with 34 goals in 36 games and was named the most valuable player.

In the playoffs against Victoria, Stewart played defense—and led all scorers with six goals in eight games. Montreal won the Cup that year—the last time that Stan-

ley Cup competition involved teams outside the NHL.

Seibert and Stewart both left the team in 1932. Benedict also dropped out of the picture. Alex Connell, who had set a record in 1926-1927 of 446 minutes 6 seconds without allowing a goal (while he himself turned in six shutouts), came out of retirement to join the Maroons in 1934. Despite the layoff, he played well for the Maroons, and the club won the Cup. He retired as a champion after that season.

Hard times gripped Canada and the Forum. Neither the Canadiens nor the Maroons attracted substantial crowds, and the Maroons were dropped so the Canadiens might live. There were, after all, more French fans than English fans in the city.

New York Americans

Most fans in New York City are unaware that their first NHL team was not the Rangers, but the Americans. The team, owned by rumrunner Bill Dwyer, was actually the storm-tossed Hamilton (Ontario) team moved south.

The Americans never finished first and never won a Cup. They had a reputation for picking up players who had seen better days, and at one time or another had Edward ("Eddie") W. Shore, Clarence H. ("Hap") Day, Harvey ("Busher") Jackson, Charles W. Conacher, and Dave ("Sweeney") Shriner. Even if the Americans had never brought hockey to New York, and hadn't acquired these name players, their place still would be secure in the history of the city—for on December 15, 1925, they were part of the inaugural sporting event at the second arena known as Madison Square Garden (the building which supplanted the original one situated opposite Madison Square Park).

The Americans' opponents at the opening were the Montreal Canadiens. The occasion meant much to Canada, for New Yorkers were to see a Canadian team play for the first time. The Canadian governor-general sent his Foot Guards to parade on the ice in their bright red uniforms. Earlier in the day they had marched along Broadway with New York's Mayor-elect James J. Walker. Mayor John F. Hylan and Walker were at the opening game, along with 17,-000 fans. The Foot Guards preceded the Canadiens on the ice, and the West Point Marching Band preceded the Americans, creating an international spectacle few New York sports fans had ever witnessed. The Canadiens won the subsequent game, 3-1, and the final goal was rapped in for the visitors by Howie Morenz. It was entirely appropriate. Morenz, known as the "Babe Ruth of Hockey," had done much to make New Yorkers aware of the sport.

He was one of the first hockey players whose fame had spread from Canada to the United States.

Those who played for Dwyer insisted he never tried anything dishonest with his club, but a recurring rumor has it that in 1933 a Dwyer lieutenant was made the goal judge for a game against Detroit. Because of heavy betting by Dwyer on his club, the judge was allegedly told to signal a goal for any New York shot that even approached the cage. After one such non-goal, the light flashed. Alex Connell, Detroit's goalie, punched the goal judge in the nose.

Dave Schriner (center) of Americans scores against Cecil (Tiny) Thompson of Bruins. At left is Eddie Shore of Boston.

(UPI)

Ching Johnson (right) and Earl Robertson, Americans' goalie, watch teammate Happy Day about to clear puck against Bruins.

(UPI)

Connell was immediately surrounded by angry fans. The goalie, escorted by a hundred policemen and two detectives, was eventually led safely back to his hotel, and guarded until he returned to Detroit.

Since not all goal judges ruled in their favor, the Americans continued to decline. For years they had been equated with the Brooklyn Dodgers in incompetence. So in 1941 management set up an office in Brooklyn and renamed the team the Brooklyn Americans. Nothing helped, though, and after the 1941-1942 season the Americans bowed out of ice hockey.

Six teams remained—the Rangers, the Canadiens, the Maple Leafs, the Red Wings, the Bruins, and the Black Hawks. There were no further changes until 1967, when the league expanded to 12 teams in the greatest single-season eruption of any professional sports league. Many maintained that ice hockey was finally catching up with the rest of professional sports. Basketball, baseball and football had expanded. But it had been forty years since ice hockey had expanded. It was decided that, after all those years, it was time to do so again.

CHAPTER III

The Dynasties

Boston Bruins

There is a reverence for history in Boston, and hockey violence is one of the town's great traditions. The fierceness began in the Thirties—and the fans of the Seventies relish history repeating itself.

As the National Hockey League's first United States representative, Boston has always had a special niche in the sport's history. When it entered the League in 1924 its future was uncertain. Despite the best efforts of the owner and manager, the Bruins were an incompetent squad.

The man who brought hockey to Boston was Charles F. Adams, a supermarket tycoon and hockey aficionado. He had played some, himself, but enjoyed the game primarily as a spectator. Whenever a good amateur contest was scheduled in Boston, Adams was sure to attend. Although he had considered that it might be pleasant and prestigious to own a team, he wasn't convinced that there was money to be derived from it. A trip to a Stanley Cup game in Montreal changed his mind. He was overwhelmed with enthusiasm, and struck by the zeal that fans in Montreal demonstrated. The fact that the fans also paid their way in impressed him, too.

Adams astounded his Canadian colleagues by hiring Arthur Howey Ross as general manager and coach of the new club, called the Bruins. Ross, one of the great players, had always revolted against authority, and was responsible for causing more turmoil during his playing years than any other competitor. He had threatened to form his own league, and had held out for more money. Now he was joining management.

Although opposing management had always regarded him as oddball, Ross had the respect of other players, so when he began to form the Bruins, he found many amateur players who would willingly turn professional to play for him. Looking for players, he journeyed to the Canadian west coast, to the north, and to the provinces in the east. But, to his dismay, he discovered that he couldn't get most of the players he really wanted—they were already under contract.

Luckily for Ross, he was able to acquire some name players from the PCHA and the WCHL because those western leagues were in a tight-money situation and it made sense for them to rid themselves of some of their high-salaried performers. Ross also hired six amateurs. Perhaps the only player anyone in the United States had ever heard of was Spunk Sparrow.

Predictably, the Bruins played like a rag-tag team, capturing only two of their first 15 games. They suffered through an 11-game losing streak, considering themselves lucky when they could score two goals a game and hold their opponents to four. In that first campaign, they finished last with one of the poorest marks in league history, winning six games and dropping 24. Since then, no NHL team has won so few games. Adams, however, had faith in Ross. Indeed, Ross remained with the Bruins for 30 seasons, finally leaving in 1953.

In the team's second year, Ross rebuilt the club he had formed only a year earlier —and the results were dramatic. In the expanded 36-game schedule, the Bruins won 17 games, lost 15 and tied four. Five starters were replaced, and Ross's great amateur experiment paid dividends: Carson Cooper and Jimmy Herberts, whom he had persuaded to turn pro, finished second and third, respectively, among the goal-scorers.

Another former amateur was the goalie, Charles Stewart. He played 35 games, turned in six shutouts, and permitted an average of only 2.3 goals a game. With Sprague Cleghorn anchoring the defense, the Bruins gave every indication that they were about to become a dynasty. In the second half of their second season they won 13 of 18 games.

Then Edward Shore came along. Virtually every sports dynasty has been built around one man, and for the Bruins it was Shore, one of a number of gifted players who became available because of the demise of the Patricks' league. Adams acquired Shore after some complicated financial maneuvering. Apparently, Adams advanced much of the $250,000 the NHL needed to buy out the western hockey leagues. After receiving Shore and several other players, Adams and Ross peddled the other players to other teams. So, for all practical purposes, Shore cost the Bruins only $15,000.

Eddie Shore was a marvel of brute strength. At six feet, weighing 180 pounds,

he was lean and hard. Some old-timers declare that Ross was the first rushing defenseman. But it was Shore who brought the style to its peak.

The most outrageous Shore legend reveals not only his extraordinary toughness, but also his desire and will—and ability. Shore probably embroidered the story over the years, but even if only half of it is true, it is quite a tale. It began one stormy, snowy night in Boston, with Shore on his way to the station to board the team train for a game at Montreal the next night. The cabdriver got stuck in traffic, and Shore missed his train.

The only other way that Shore could get to Montreal was by car. A friend offered one with a chauffeur. They drove through the night, stopping repeatedly to clean the windshield, since the wipers had been ripped off their hinges. The car skidded into a ditch at one point and Shore somehow managed to roll it back on the road. After ten hours, the chauffeur was so distraught that he refused to drive any more. Shore took over. Fifteen hours or so later, Shore arrived in Montreal. "I'm going to sleep for a few hours," he advised Ross. "I want you to wake me up for the game. If I refuse to wake up, throw a pail of cold water on me, slap my face, do anything to get me up." Ross, surprised at the mere presence of Shore, was content to let Shore sleep until the team was about to leave for the arena. Still groggy, Shore went to the rink and put on his uniform, insisting that he would play. Reluctantly, Ross put Shore in. The Bruins won, 1-0. It was Shore who scored the goal.

Shore had another memorable night in Montreal some years later. The Maroons' terrors were the trio that composed the "S" Line—"Babe" Siebert, "Hooley" Smith and Nelson Stewart. In addition to giving Shore a broken nose, facial stitches, body bruises and a black eye, the three also gave

Bobby Orr in mid-air after halting rush by Montreal's Frank Mahovlich in 1971 Cup playoff game while Gerry Cheevers protects Boston goal.

Boston's Derek Sanderson flips over after body check by Bob Plager of Blues in 1970 Stanley Cup playoff final.

Atlanta goalie Phil Myre fails to block shot by Boston's Fred O'Donnell.

yl Apps of Penguins (on top) and Don Awrey f Bruins become entangled in pursuit of puck.

Shore verbal insults. But Shore continued to play. When the game ended, Adams walked over to Shore and handed him a check for $500. "Use this as a bandage," Adams told him.

With Shore, the Bostonians finished second in the American Division in the 1926-1927 season, then captured the divisional title four seasons in a row. In 1929, the Bruins won their first Cup. That was also the year of their first outstanding line—the "Dynamite Trio." The three were Cooney Weiland, the center; Dutch Gainor, the left wing; and Aubrey V. ("Dit") Clapper on the right side. Clapper was to be the first NHL player to last 20 years, retiring in 1947. It wasn't until 1966 that any other player could make that claim. The Bruins also were blessed in their first Stanley Cup year with the arrival of C. ("Tiny") Thompson, the goalie. Thompson, who posted two shutouts over the Canadiens in Cup play, would win the Vezina Trophy (for permitting the fewest goals) four times over the next decade.

With all this talent on the ice, Ross decided to abandon his coaching duties. He remained as general manager, but appointed Frank Patrick as coach, following the 1933-1934 campaign. After two seasons, in which Patrick led the team to a first and second, Ross returned to the bench. Now he had a new attacking line—the "Kraut Line." The members—Milt Schmidt, Bob Bauer and Woody Dumart —all were born in Kitchener, Ontario, a city that had been named Berlin before World War I. (When hostilities began, merchants in the town complained that they had difficulty selling products stamped "Made in Berlin," so the name was changed to honor Lord Horatio Kitchener, the British war hero.)

Neither the Bruins nor their fans knew it, of course, but the years before World War II were to signal the beginning of the end of contending Boston teams for nearly 30 years. They made some sparks before they went out, however. With Ross as coach, the Bruins won the Cup again in 1939. Again, Ross stepped down for two seasons, his place as coach taken by Weiland. It didn't seem to matter to the Bruins, who won the Cup again in 1941, following their fourth straight first-place finish. Schmidt, Dumart and Bauer were so formidable that they finished first, second and third, respectively, in scoring in 1940.

Although Ross remained as coach until 1945, it was apparent that things would never be the same. In the following years, Bruins' coaches came and went with alarming regularity. It took 30 years—until 1971 —for the Bruins to finish first again. It took 29 years—until 1970—for the Stanley Cup to be returned to Boston. From 1960 to 1967 the Bostonians finished last six times, and next-to-last twice.

The 1960's weren't without some benefit for the Bruins. Bobby Orr was coming of age. He was first spotted in 1961— when he was only 13 years old. Weston Adams, who inherited the club's presidency from his father, had gone to see a highly touted youngster playing for Gananoque, an Ontario club. Quite soon, though, they were watching another player—a smallish boy who appeared to have remarkable poise for someone so young.

"Say, who's that blond kid?" Adams asked one of his scouts, Wren Blair.

"His name's Orr," Blair replied.

Within a week, the Bruins met with Orr's parents, and Bobby Orr soon was a member of the Bruins' organization.

The 1966-1967 season began the Age of Orr. Bobby was only 18 years of age, the youngest player in the league. Behind the bench was Harry Sinden, the new coach, who was 35. The new general manager was Milt Schmidt, whom Sinden had replaced on the bench. Even before Orr ever played a game, it was obvious he was going to revolutionize hockey—the teen-ager refused to negotiate his contract without a lawyer! He picked a good counselor—Alan Eagleson, a prominent Torontonian who was not only director of the Players Association, but also a member of the Ontario Parliament. Rumors varied widely as to the amount of money Orr actually received. Some said that he landed a three-year contract, including a bonus, that was worth a quarter-of-a-million dollars. Certainly, no rookie had ever earned so much before! Few players in the 1960's even had a lawyer negotiate for them. The last time an amateur had caused such a front-office stir was in 1950, when Jean Beliveau was coaxed by Montreal to leave the "amateur" ranks.

Orr's first season was a rebuilding year for the Bruins, and they finished last. Orr was named the second-team all-star, although he had played in only 61 games. At the end of the season, Harry Howell won the James Norris Trophy as best defenseman, and said with a chuckle, "I'm glad I won it now—no one else but Orr will win it for the next 20 years."

Despite their last-place finish, the Bruins continued to draw attendance. Surprisingly, they outdrew the Celtics during the 1960's, although the Celtics won one basketball championship after the other. Finally, the hockey fans had even more reason to turn out. Before the 1967-1968 season, Schmidt engineered a deal with Chicago that was to haunt the Black Hawks and help put the Bruins on top.

Phil Esposito, who had lived in the shadows as Bobby Hull's center at Chicago, Ken Hodge, a strapping right wing, and Fred Stanfield, a young center, joined the Bruins in a trade that sent Gilles Marotte, Pit Martin and Jack Norris to the Hawks.

With these new scorers, plus Orr and another defenseman known as Terrible Ted Green (or "Greenie the Meanie"), the Bruins finished third in the 1967-1968 season. They quickly became known as the Big Bad Bruins as they rumbled over anyone in their way, throwing the first punch and the last punch.

"For years, people stepped on us," said Harry Sinden, "so why is everyone getting so excited just because we hit back? I didn't hear anyone defending us when we were down." The Bruins were the biggest and strongest and toughest squad in the league. Schmidt had told his scouts, "If they can fit through the door, I don't want 'em."

Derek ("Turk") Sanderson also joined the Bruins in 1967, and, like Orr, was named rookie of the year. An infuriating player with a mischievous flair, he was especially good at killing penalties. Often, the opposition was afraid to bear in with him on the ice. His quick stick could poke a puck free from an attacker and convert it into a short-handed goal.

The nucleus finally led the Bruins to the Cup in 1970, with Orr having one of the most incredible seasons in history. Before he came along, the record for goals by a defenseman was 20. He got 33 in the 1969-1970 season, added a record (for any player) of 87 assists, and amassed 120 points!

Orr's point total nearly doubled the record for defensemen which he had set the year before. His display even overshadowed—if that was possible—the accomplishments of Phil Esposito. In the 1968-1969 campaign, Esposito had become the first player to reach the hundred-point plateau. The highest point total previously achieved had been 97. Esposito got 126.

As expected, the Bruins finished first during the 1970-1971 season, even though Harry Sinden had quit. Sinden wanted more money than the Bruins were prepared to give. Tom Johnson, a quiet, or-

derly pipe-smoker given to wearing bow ties, took over the raucous Bruins. The Bostonians wound up with more goals than any team had scored before, and Esposito amassed 152 points, including a record-shattering 76 goals. But the Bruins were ousted in the first round of the playoffs. The 1971-1972 campaign was different. Not only did Boston sweep through the regular season, but it took the Cup. A dynasty appeared ready to supplant the Canadiens. But strange things happened to the club in the off-season. The WHA came along and lured away Derek Sanderson with a $2.65-million package deal, snared John McKenzie for $100,000 a year, and took the No. 1 goalie, Gerry Cheevers, for $166,000 annually. In addition, Green, nearing the end of his career, also went to the new league for more money. To compound difficulties, the Bruins gave up Dan Bouchard, a top-flight minor-league goalie, and Ed Westfall, a proven forward and penalty-killer, in the expansion draft. Suddenly, several key members of the dynasty were gone. Despite the losses, the Bruins still had what no one else could boast of—Orr and Esposito.

They got back Sanderson midway through the 1972-1973 season, but Johnson was dismissed during a losing streak and replaced by Armand ("Beb") Guidolin. The Bruins' "dynasty" suddenly had ended, and housecleaning was in order.

Phil Esposito of Bruins skates in as Gilles Meloche of Seals controls puck.

(Al Ruelle)

Chicago Black Hawks

Since they first suited up in 1926, the Hawks have had the most curious mixture of towering figures and laughable clowns of any team. Their "ups" have been sensational. And their protracted stretches of "downs" have resembled comic opera. Fittingly, most of their heroics took place in cavernous Chicago Stadium, the biggest arena in the NHL. They boast the distinction of being the only club to rise from last to first in successive seasons, of finishing atop the East Division one year and then leading the West Division the next. Looking at the power-packed Chicago line-up of recent years, it is difficult to imagine a time when the Hawks were ridiculously inept, as they were, for most of their history.

Their early failures have been blamed on the "Muldoon Curse," a fascinating legend that was probably the concoction of a sportswriter. But, fact or fiction, the curse really seemed to work. The legend has it that Pete Muldoon, the Hawks' first coach, was so angered at his dismissal after one year at the helm that he hexed the Hawks constantly by intoning, "The Black Hawks will never finish first." Since they didn't finish first over the next 40 years, who could deny that the curse existed?

It was Major Frederic McLaughlin—one of Chicago's men-about-town, former war hero, stellar polo player, and husband of entertainment star Irene Castle—who first brought big-league hockey to the city. He paid Lester Patrick more than $100,000 for the entire Portland team, which Mc-Laughlin hoped would form the nucleus of his new Black Hawks, grandly named after his World War I battalion. McLaughlin didn't permit his ignorance of hockey to stand in the way. He made the first of his headstrong moves by hiring Muldoon as coach and Bill Tobin as his general man-ager. Although he never did find players who could win consistently, Tobin remained as manager for 30 years, outlasting a dizzying succession of coaches who just couldn't win with the players Tobin provided.

Bad luck, if not the curse, indeed plagued the Hawks. They finished third in their first campaign, aided by four players—"Babe" Dye, James D. ("Dick") Irvin, Hugh Lehman and George Hay—who were to make the Hockey Hall of Fame. But that didn't satisfy the major; he dismissed Muldoon and hired Barney Stanley. The streak of bizarre misfortune followed. Dye broke his leg in a practice session, and his career as a scorer was over. Hay was traded to Detroit (where he would become the fifth highest scorer in the league that season). Irvin fractured his skull in the twelfth game of the season (while he was among the high scorers), ending his career. Lehman was suddenly "over the hill"—he was 40 years old, and could no longer stand the strain of goaltending. The Hawks had one bright spot, however. They had brought up a young goalie named Charles ("Chuck") Gardiner to replace Hugh Lehman. He lasted for seven years, becoming one of the great playoff goalies —a two-time all-star and a two-time Vezina Trophy winner. Then, in 1934, at the peak of his career, he died of a brain tumor.

Stanley didn't even last one season. He was replaced midway through it by Lehman. The revolving door for Chicago coaches was gaining momentum. Although they continued to miss gaining first place, the Hawks soared to the Cup after eight seasons, in 1934. By then, they had eliminated ten coaches. One of the players was asked which coach was the worst. "I'd say it was a photo-finish among six of them," he replied.

During the 1932-1933 season, there

Tony Esposito goes to his left to smother shot by Lew Morrison of Flyers.

(Wide World)

were no fewer than three Chicago coaches. In 1931-1932, there were two, including Irvin. The major had Irvin introduce a military concept to hockey: the thinking that enough fresh troops will overwhelm the opposition. Irvin thus became one of the first coaches to develop rapid line changes—when one trio tired, another would take its place. That is precisely the way ice hockey is played today. Irvin, how-

ever, didn't have competent "troops." He had many players, but few of them could get the job done. Irvin was dismissed. Later, he was to gain coaching fame with the formidable Montreal teams.

Even Tommy Gorman, who coached the Hawks to their first Cup victory in 1934, wasn't rehired the following season. Bill Stewart, who led the team to their second Cup in 1938, was replaced midway through the next campaign. The season as a whole was such a disaster that Major McLaughlin began a desperate search for ways to bring in fans. Finally, he instructed Tobin to hire United States players and field a complete lineup of Americans—perhaps fans would come to see "their own kind." Tobin demonstrated why he had a record for longevity under the major when he went along with the scheme. But after only one victory in three weeks, the idea was abandoned.

That 1938-1939 season began a 20-year period in which the Hawks finished last 10 times, missed the playoffs 14 times, and finished as high as third only once. The major apparently came to accept defeat. He retained Paul Thompson as coach from the 1938-1939 season through the 1943-1944 campaign. McLaughlin died in 1944, and the Hawks, for better or worse, were practically without direction.

The ownership of the team was in doubt, and the league was concerned that the Chicago players wouldn't get paid. In fact, the NHL took over the operation. The franchise was saved in 1946 when James D. Norris took command with Arthur Wirtz as his partner. The Norris and Wirtz families had one thing in common: enormous wealth. Both loved ice hockey; and Norris had been an amateur player in his younger days. Norris set out to prove that money could buy hockey happiness. Over the next ten years he probably sank two million dollars into the team. But it takes more than money to acquire players; it also takes influence. Norris had enough of that, too—his family owned a share of the Detroit Red Wings, and he was a substantial stockholder in Madison Square Garden, as well as a prime figure in thoroughbred racing. He could do favors for such important people as Conn Smythe, owner of the Maple Leafs, who was also involved in horse racing.

It took years for Norris's investments to reap dividends. Perhaps even more important than the players he acquired was the acquisition of Tommy Ivan as general manager in 1954. Ivan had just led the Detroit Red Wings to their sixth straight first-place finish as their coach. At Chicago, he became both coach and general manager. He started out by shoring up the weakened farm system—concentrating on the minor leagues as training grounds for players. Soon he had a fellow named Bobby Hull playing for him in the minors, along with Stan Mikita and Pierre Piolote. In 1957, Hull joined the Hawks at age 18. Ivan engineered a trade with his former bosses at Detroit that also brought Glenn Hall to Chicago to play goal. That 1957-1958 campaign signaled an end to 20 years of Chicago ineptitude. The Hawks were ready to fly!

A decade of prosperity began in 1958. Ken Wharram, probably the fastest skater in the game, joined the club, as did Stan Mikita. The nucleus of superstars was formed. In later years, the star syndrome was to be blamed by some observers for the Hawks' failure to finish first, although the big names made the club perennial powerhouses. Ivan left the coaching ranks, though not the team, after one and a half seasons, replaced by Rudy Pilous, who had coached Hull, Mikita and Pilote in the minors. Not all players were ecstatic about Pilous's ability. Eric Nesterenko remarked with a sneer, "Pilous couldn't coach a girls' softball team." Pilous lasted until 1963, when Ivan, a dapper and outgoing sort, hired Billy Reach Reay, a taciturn, unemotional man, as coach. Reay was to last longer than any coach in the club's history.

Hull was the focus of the team. Combining raw strength with unusual speed, he became the most feared shooter since Maurice ("Rocket") Richard of Montreal. But not even the Rocket could shoot as hard or score as consistently from 60 feet out. In his third season, by the time he was 21, Hull led the league in goals and total points. With his blond hair and dynamic skating style he came across as the most dashing figure in the sport. Scientists studied his physique. They measured his skating speed, the velocity of his slap shot, and the rapidity with which he released it. They came to some startling conclusions. He was the perfect physical specimen, said one doctor. His speed approached 30 miles an hour, and only one or two other individuals could match it. But it was ultimately his shot, timed at nearly 120 miles an hour, that brought him acclaim. Most of the other players tested couldn't reach a hundred miles an hour in their attempts.

It didn't take long for opposing coaches to map strategies designed to stop Hull, a left wing. Thus, the "shadow" came about. The shadow usually was an opposing right wing whose job was easily defined: to stop Hull. For some, it meant doing it by any means necessary. To others it became a true sporting challenge. Some of the finest players of the 1960's and 1970's were assigned to shadow Hull, including Claude Provost of the Montreal Canadiens, Bob Nevin and Ron Stewart of the Rangers, Eddie Westfall of the Bruins, and the well-traveled Bryan Watson, the most unnerving one of them all. Hull, in a rare display of off-the-ice temper, once labelled Watson "an animal" for his no-holds-barred tactics. Another rough shadow was the Canadiens' John Ferguson, one of the few who weren't afraid to fight Hull if the situation called for it.

Despite the shadows, Hull remained one of the game's most successful players, and is largely credited with helping expansion come about. Without doubt, he was the most famous ice hockey player in North America. From 1960 to 1969, he led the goal-scorers seven times. He became the third man to amass 50 goals in a season, and the first man to do it more than once. During his playing career, he scored 50 or more goals four times.

Hull was fortunate in one respect. He didn't have to worry about Glenn Hall, the goalie, stopping him. Hall joined the Hawks following two outstanding seasons for Detroit, where he had replaced famed Terry Sawchuk.

Glenn Hall's face reflected the agony of goalkeeping—it was perpetually sad. His nervousness was apparent before most games, when he would suffer stomach cramps, but when the puck was dropped, Hall played, according to one observer, "as though a mouse were running up and down his spine." His erratic leaps and splits usually kept the puck out. He led the league in shutouts for four consecutive seasons and set a record for netminders of 502 straight games played—despite the jittery feelings he often showed and spoke about.

"Sometimes I just feel like standing in the middle of my farm and screaming, 'Nuts to hockey!'" he said.

Hall was supremely important to the reorganized Hawks. The club's defense was not exceptional, since most of its energies were poured into scoring with the game's most feared collection of heavy gunners. Hall was the last line of defense, and he guarded the cage as well as (and probably better than) any goalie of his time.

Although Mikita never scored 50 goals, and never became the hero-figure that Hull was, at least one general manager said of the little center, "If I had one man to build a team around, I'd pick Mikita."

Guile and cunning, coupled with remarkable quickness, elevated Mikita to the forefront of the centers in the National Hockey League. Not too tall (5 feet 9 inch-

Bobby Hull reaches milestone—his 600th goal—in 15th NHL season as he fires puck past Bobby Orr (on knees) and Boston goaltender Gerry Cheevers in March 25, 1972 game. The only player to score more goals was Gordie Howe of Red Wings who made 786 in a 25-year career.

es), weighing 165 pounds, Stan Mikita used techniques he had learned as a small boy, when he opposed larger kids, by making everything work for him.

He was only 19 when he became a big-league regular. Within a few years he became the leading point-maker in the league, but he also accumulated 119 minutes in penalties. He displayed an uncanny ability to spot his wings, even if they were behind him, and his perfectly placed passes led to so many goals that he led the NHL in assists for three straight seasons. Mikita's contributions to the sport may be overshadowed by a freak accident that led to the curved sticks that hockey players now use. Who knows how many hundreds of former players broke the blades of their sticks during practice? But Mikita was the first to translate the broken stick into a new weapon—the curved blade. It happened one morning after he accidentally bent the blade. He took the deformed stick onto the ice, and aimed a few shots at the net. To his surprise, the puck acted like a knuckleball: it fluttered, it dipped, it rose,

it curved. Hull was watching with interest. Mikita ordered a few specially curved sticks from the manufacturer, and Hull did the same. In Hull's hands, the curved stick revolutionized the game. Now, coupled with strength and velocity, the curved stick made Hull's shot even more dangerous by making it erratic. Mikita mastered all the intricacies of the curved stick, and was one of the few players who could make pinpoint passes with it. As his skill increased, Mikita's penalty minutes decreased. "I learned I didn't have to prove anything just because I was small," he said. In short order, he won the Lady Byng Trophy for his clean play.

This collection of stars still couldn't elevate the Hawks to the very top. The Muldoon Curse held fast, even though the Hawks had five players on the first all-star team in the 1963-1964 season. That was the disturbing thing about the Hawks for their fans—the club was a constant contender, but could not gain better than second place.

The curse was finally broken at the end

of the 1966-1967 season, when the Hawks finished on top of the standings for the first time. Coach Reay had insisted that the club's heavy scorers concentrate on defense. Reay also instituted the two-goalie system, which was to become standard a few years later. He alternated Hall with Denis DeJordy, so each goalie was well-rested for the nerve-jangling play. That first championship also marked the end of another era. The following season expansion took place, in which the new West Division was formed. So the Hawks, who had never before finished first in the NHL, became the last club to lead the league under its original structure.

As suddenly as they gained the top rank, the team then began to decline. The following season the Hawks slumped to fourth place as their defense fell apart. Hall was gone in the expansion draft. The deal with Boston was a disaster, with only Pit Martin delivering among the new players. In the 1968-1969 campaign, despite Hull's record 58 goals, the Hawks went even lower, finishing last. It was obvious to Tommy Ivan that sweeping changes would have to be made.

No one expected the revolution that Tommy Ivan brought about. First, he shocked traditionalists by bringing up three players from the University of Denver. They included Keith Magnuson and Cliff Koroll. Ivan also acquired another youngster, Tony Esposito, younger brother of Phil, from the Canadiens as a goalie.

The new-look Hawks turned into winners. Magnuson led the belting, and Pat Stapleton was the rock on defense. Hull, who had held out over a contract dispute, rejoined the team and played in the new defensive style that Reay insisted on. Mikita, too, sacrificed firepower in an attempt to cut down goals.

Esposito was the big surprise. By mid-season he had turned in eight shutouts. He was a fluke, his critics cried, but he held firm. Late in the season, Ivan engineered another major deal. This one didn't backfire. He got Bill White, a defenseman, and Gerry Desjardins, a goalie, from Los Angeles, where the two were constantly complaining against management. DeJordy went to Los Angeles, along with Gilles Marotte, who had originally come to the Hawks from Boston. The race was so close that, as the season moved into the final weekend, the Hawks had to defeat the Canadiens twice in order to clinch first place. But they did it. They became the first club to leap from last to first in consecutive seasons, with Tony Esposito getting a record 15 shutouts.

The 1969-1970 season also marked the end of the Hawks' tenure among the established clubs in the East Division. Just the year before it had been agreed that the Hawks needed help because they were playing so badly. To help the Hawks, it was decided that for the 1970-1971 season they would be moved to the West Division, home of the weaker expansion teams. No one even imagined that the Hawks would enter the division as champions.

That is precisely what happened, though. The Hawks dominated the new division from the beginning, and ran away with the West Division title in 1970-1971, 1971-1972, and again in 1972-1973. Thus, after failing to finish first in 40 years, the Hawks became a team that captured the top rung five times in the next seven years.

Ironically, Hull, who had been the major reason for the team's success, then became one of the major (if not the most important) creators of the WHA. When the Hawks failed to meet his salary demands, he jumped leagues for his famous million-dollar cash bonus and long-term contract. Bitterness followed his move to the rival league. The Hawks had lost a player that no one could hope to replace.

Detroit Red Wings

One memorable seven-year interval overshadows all the other years the Red Wings have spent in the National Hockey League. From the 1948-1949 season through to the 1954-1955 season, the Detroiters finished first for seven consecutive seasons. When they were on top, their dynasty was favorably compared to that of the then invincible New York Yankees.

"We're not the Yankees of ice hockey," protested Jack Adams, the Red Wings' general manager, whenever that comparison reached his ears. "The Yankees are the Red Wings of baseball!"

Few could deny it. The Detroit club of those years included at least two players who were subsequently considered the finest ever to play their positions: Gordie Howe, the right wing, and Terry Sawchuck, the goalie. In addition, there were Sid Abel at center and Ted Lindsay at left wing. During the championship streak, the Wings captured the Cup four times. Indeed, throughout those seven seasons the team finished first more times and won more Cups than in all its other years combined.

For most of those years, good and bad, Jack Adams was at the helm. The team began without him when a group of businessmen bought the Victoria Cougars for $100,000 and brought them to Detroit. Art Duncan, one of the Victoria players, also served as coach that first season, which was a disaster. The club captured only 12 of 44 games, and finished last in its division. It was to be the only last-place finish for a Detroit team until 40 years later.

Actually, the team wasn't in Detroit during its first year. The Olympia, the arena being built for them, was not yet completed, so the club played across the Detroit River, in Windsor, Ontario. The club lost more than $80,000 in its first season, when it was known as the Cougars. It

had three players who later made the Hockey Hall of Fame: Frank Frederickson, Frank Foyston and Frank Walker. But by that time all were in their mid-30's and their careers would end within a few seasons. Their peak had been reached years before, and so the Cougars wound up with a team of has-beens.

Charles Hughes, the team's president, demanded a winner for the 1927-1928 season, the club's first in the new arena. Frank Calder, the league's president, recommended Jack Adams as the man to mold the Cougars into a winning team. Adams' playing career had just ended, at the age of 32. He had been a Pacific Coast League scoring champion, and had ended his playing career with the Ottawa Senators, who won the Cup in 1927.

"When I walked in to see Hughes," Jack Adams later recalled, "I was at an advantage. He had finished last and lost a ton of money. I had just played for a Stanley Cup winner. I told him he needed me more than I needed him. He agreed."

The remarkable association—Adams and Detroit—had begun. He would coach the club for 20 years, and serve as general manager for 35. During his days with Detroit, the team finished first 12 times and captured seven Cups.

In the first year of Jack Adams's reign, the Cougars showed a profit, due in part to the publicity given the new stadium and the team's dramatic improvement to a .500 record. In the club's third season, it qualified for playoffs. The club was still erratic, though, and fans began to turn away. Financial problems increased during the 1929-1930 season, when the business depression hit. Attendance slumped to three thousand fans a game. Adams, a tireless promoter, was faced with a really difficult task: bringing fans (most of whom had never seen a hockey game) to watch a losing club at major-league admission prices. He arranged an extensive schedule of dinners, and made himself available to "spread the word." His pockets bulged with tickets, which he sold wherever he went. When he couldn't sell them, he gave them away. One night in 1930 the club staged an exhibition for charity: fans would pay what they could afford, the expenses would go to the club, and the profits would go to the charity. One farmer stood outside, unable to make a contribution. But he mentioned that he had five pounds of potatoes in his truck. Adams took the potatoes and let the farmer in.

To stimulate interest, Jack Adams ran a contest to change the club's name before the 1930-1931 season began. The winning name was declared to be the Falcons. Despite the new name, though, the same old faces were there; Adams didn't have the funds to acquire players. The Falcons again missed the playoffs.

Spirits sagged in the club, and not even Jack Adams's blustery attempts at humor could perk them up. One unhappy player told Adams, "I'm going to open a chain of hot dog stands and put them at all the train stops. With the kind of food you're giving the guys, they'll buy from me and I'll be rich." Even Adams could see the lunacy of his situation. He recalled later, "We were so poor that if Howie Morenz [the greatest scorer of those days] were available for $1.98, we couldn't have afforded him."

By the end of the 1933 season, Adams's manipulations and trades had elevated the Wings to second place. They simply needed new impetus to get them over the top, and they got it when James D. Norris bought the team. Norris, the multi-millionaire grain merchant who loved hockey, yearned to own a team. He had even bought Chicago Stadium, hoping to buy

Detroit's Gordie Howe between Hawks' Chico Maki (left) and Keith Magnuson.

Marcel Dionne (center) and Bill Collins of Detroit chase puck as Bert Marshall of Seals checks Dionne in Olympia Stadium game.

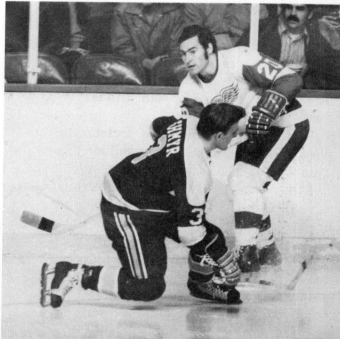

Mickey Redmond of Red Wings is hip-checked by Paul Shmyr of Seals.

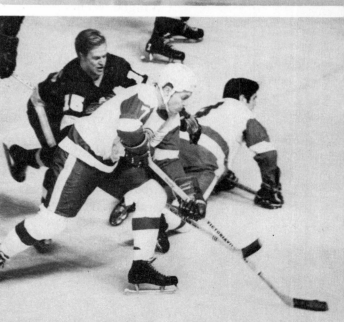

Detroit's Red Berenson, with puck on tip of stick, is pursued by Juha Widding of Kings. On the ice is Detroit's Arnie Brown.

the Black Hawks (which he did later, in 1946). Meanwhile, Arthur M. Wirtz, himself a millionaire, was majority owner of the Olympia. Wirtz and Norris made a trade. Wirtz took over Chicago Stadium, and Norris the Olympia. Norris also became the Falcons' president.

Adams was unaware of the negotiations. He was concerned about whether he would even have a club with which to start the 1933-1934 season. There were strong rumors that the Falcons would be unable to continue.

One morning Adams walked into his office. His secretary announced excitedly, "There's a call from Chicago. The new owner wants to talk to you."

Adams, stunned, replied, "New owner? Who?" He refused to believe anyone would be foolhardy enough to want to take over the club.

"Mr. James Norris," the secretary replied. "You know—the grain millionaire."

Jack Adams picked up the phone. "Adams?" said the voice on the other end. "Be with me at my banker's today when I take over your lousy club."

That was the first time the pair spoke, but it was the beginning of a long and satisfying relationship based on mutual respect. Later that day Norris informed Adams that the club would be renamed the Red Wings. Norris fondly recalled playing for a club called the Winged Wheelers when he had been a youngster. He thought it would be appropriate in Detroit to have a wheel for an emblem, and he thereupon decided that the symbol should be a red wheel with a wing.

"That ought to make Henry Ford happy," added Norris.

Norris made another decision that first day. Adams would continue to head the operation for a year "on probation."

There was immediate and joyous reaction among the players when Norris took over. Now there would be money available to insure their pay. Norris dispatched the Olympia's huge debt, and the players were satisfied with their contracts for their first season, 1933-1934, as Red Wings. To celebrate, they finished first, gaining their first league championship.

Their star was an impressive scorer named Ebenezer ("Ebbie") Goodfellow, who was to be honored in the Hockey Hall of Fame. Goodfellow was such an outstanding athlete that Adams converted him to defense the following season, in a move to shore up the club's weak spot. Goodfellow made the conversion in fine fashion, but there weren't enough other quality defenders, so the Red Wings fell to fourth place. Adams knew he needed a scorer. One was available—a fellow named Syd Howe of the St. Louis Eagles. The Eagles were in desperate need of cash. Howe, no relation to Gordie, could be obtained for $35,000, an enormous sum during those lean years. Norris, never one to scrimp when it came to hockey, instructed Adams to get Howe. They didn't know it then, of course, but the name Howe would become synonymous with Detroit. From 1935 to 1971, 37 straight seasons, there would be a Howe on top in their line-up.

Once they got Syd, there was no stopping the Wings. They finished first and then went on to take their first Cup. To prove that it was no fluke, they performed the same amazing feat the following season. They were the first club to finish first and gain the Cup in consecutive seasons.

His club appeared so strong that Adams made no changes at all. He must have imagined that his stars—which included Hec Kilrea, Johnny Sorrell and "Mud" Bruneteau—could go on and on. He quickly learned that this wasn't true. In the 1937-1938 season, the defending champion Red Wings lost more than twice as many games as they won, and they missed the playoffs. "I'll never make that mistake again," vowed Adams, whose new philosophy was: Trade the stars before they're too old to bring anything in return.

Adams also realized he would need a constant stream of younger players to keep a club at the top. He is credited with becoming the first ice hockey executive to start an extensive farm (or minor-league) system. But it took time. While he was waiting for it to develop, the Wings went through a five-year period in which they lost more games than they won. It did appear that they would be able to salvage a Stanley Cup at the end of the streak, though—they made it to the finals of the 1942 playoffs. They won the first three games of the best-of-seven series against the Toronto Maple Leafs. They led with 15 minutes remaining in the fourth, and presumably final, game. But the Wings, despite their 4-3 lead, lost to the Leafs. At the end of the game Jack Adams skated across the ice to engage in an argument with Referee Mel Harwood, contending that Harwood's officiating had cost the Wings the game. Three of his players also argued with Harwood, and Adams finally threw a punch at the referee. It was a costly gesture. Adams was suspended for the remainder of the series. Disheartened after losing this important game, and then playing without their coach, the Red Wings went into an incredible nosedive. They dropped the next three games and lost the Cup—becoming the only team in league history to lose the Cup after winning the first three games of the series.

During the World War II years, Jack Adams still got his team into the playoffs. He had lost one of his stars, Sid Abel, a left wing, to the armed forces. But Syd Howe was still on tap, and on February 3, 1944, he turned in the greatest one-game performance of the new era, scoring six goals in the game against the Rangers, a record that wouldn't be equaled for 24 years. Syd Howe's last season was 1946, when Gordie Howe came along. Abel was back from the service, and Ted Lindsay was a youngster on the squad. The beginning of the dynasty that would soon rule the hockey world was taking shape. That 1946-1947 season was the last one for Jack Adams as coach. The team finished fourth, and Adams turned the coaching chores over to Tommy Ivan, whom he had carefully groomed and brought along in the Wings' ever-widening farm system. In his first season, Ivan conceived the "Production Line," uniting Howe, Abel and Lindsay, which would ultimately become one of the most effective lines in the sport's history. The Red Wings finished second under Ivan in his first year, and then began their fabulous run of seven consecutive first-place finishes.

They were joined by Red Kelly, a clean, unselfish defenseman, and eventually by Terry Sawchuk, the magnificent goalie.

But it was Gordie Howe who was the heart of the club. (Twenty-five years after his first appearance he was still among the leading scorers in the league.) He had joined the Detroiters when he was only eighteen. One day in training camp, after he learned he had made the club, he knocked on Adams's door.

"You were supposed to give me something special if I made the club, Mr. Adams," Howe told him.

Adams immediately concluded that young Howe was going to be difficult when it came to signing a contract. Suspicious, he asked Howe what he wanted.

"The team jacket you promised," said Howe.

Howe earned it over the years. He broke Rocket Richard's mark for lifetime goals by 242, amassing 786 by the time he retired in 1971. He led the league six times in scoring, including four straight years.

Ted Lindsay (center) of Red Wings fights Leafs' Allan Stanley for puck as Detroit goalie Terry Sawchuk prepares to defend against possible shot.

He was voted into the league's first-team or second-team All-Stars 15 straight seasons and 21 times in his 25 years. Yet he was a team player in the best sense of the word. One year, when he had a chance to become the second man ever to get 50 goals in a campaign, he suddenly avoided shooting as often as he might have. When Adams asked him for an explanation, Howe replied, "I'd like Abel to get 20 goals . . . whenever I see him free I'll pass the puck to him." Howe wound up with forty-nine goals that season. His ability didn't linger merely as a legend, as it does for some after their prime has passed. He worked at keeping it alive. In the 1968-1969 season, at the age of 41 and in his twenty-third season, Howe scored 44 goals and had a career high of 103 points. In his twenty-fifth season, 1970-1971, he exceeded the 20-goal mark for the twenty-second straight time.

For most of Detroit's seven championship years, Terry Sawchuk, a crewcut whiz and a brilliant student of the game, was the team's goalie. He learned how to play the various angles that shots could zero in on him, and he knew how to position his body so he could give the opposing player virtually no open space to aim for.

Terry Sawchuk's most memorable performance, for many, was in the 1952 playoffs, which the Red Wings won in eight straight games. He turned in four shutouts, a record for eight games, and permitted only five goals.

Sawchuk, Howe, Lindsay, and Kelly were products of the Detroit farm system. They were so young when they came to Detroit that Adams later liked to joke: "When I'd come home from a trip, they'd rush up to me and shout, 'Daddy—what did you bring me?'"

Ivan didn't coach the club to complete its string of seven titles in a row. After the sixth consecutive victory, following the 1953-1954 season, he joined the Black Hawks as coach. The Hawks were owned by Jim Norris, Jr., and it was no secret that the Wings and Hawks were involved in numerous deals, most of them calculated to make the Hawks more respectable. In four years the Hawks received 19 players from Detroit—*and* Ivan.

Because of the rise of the Canadiens in the late 1950's and early 1960's, and also because of several bad deals that Adams negotiated, the Red Wings sagged. In 1962, Sid Abel replaced Jack Adams as general manager, and the old man bowed out testily. Abel, who was also the coach, tried to develop younger players. But it still was Gordie Howe, teamed with another old-timer, Alex Delvecchio—and Norm Ullman, who arrived in the mid-1950's—who formed the nucleus. The Wings got an outstanding rookie in goalie Roger Crozier, who helped them

Alex Delvecchio gets his 449th goal against Gilles Meloche of Seals.

reach first place in 1964-1965. When Abel decided that coaching and managing was a bit too much, he transferred the coaching reins to Bill Gadsby, one of his best defensemen. Gadsby lasted only a little more than a season, and Abel returned to coach.

The 1970-1971 season began with Abel in the front office and another new coach on the bench—Ned Harkness, a surprise choice. Harkness had been the fabulously successful hockey coach at Cornell University, compiling one of the most enviable records in North America. Some of his theories upset the older regulars. There was

54

talk of a players' strike, and Abel refused to back up Harkness, whom Abel hadn't wanted for the job. The Red Wings hit bottom. In mid-season, the strangest turn of all took place—Abel delivered an ultimatum to management: "Harkness or me." Management stayed with Harkness. So Abel, a member of the Detroit organization since 1938, quit. Ned Harkness was elevated to the post of general manager, and a former Detroiter, Doug Barkley, was made coach. Wholesale trades followed as Harkness sought to remake a Red Wing club that he believed had grown soft and old.

The Wings fell to seventh place under the Barkley-Harkness combination, finishing last behind two brand-new expansion teams, Vancouver and Buffalo. But in the 1971-1972 season the Harkness deals paid off. John Wilson replaced Barkley as coach, and under Wilson's guidance, with the players Harkness had chosen, the Wings were in contention for a playoff berth until the final week of the season. Howe was gone along with virtually every other player who had been on the scene when Harkness arrived. It would take time to determine whether his housecleaning methods worked.

Montreal Canadiens

In a Boston dressing room in 1969, Derek Sanderson dazedly tried to understand how his club had just been eliminated from the Stanley Cup playoffs by the Montreal Canadiens. The Bruins had led until the final seconds in the first two games, but in each one the Canadiens had then tied the score and won in overtime.

"We tried to stop a dynasty," said Sanderson. "And when you do that, you need luck."

There are sports writers and fans who insist it is more than luck that is required because the Canadiens, or "Flying Frenchmen," have a certain mystique about them. Clubs have gone down to defeat at their hands, never quite understanding just how they lost. There is always a "never-too-late" quality to the Canadiens' play, and even when the opposition has a huge lead, it must wonder if the Canadiens will overcome it.

All National Hockey League teams have a measure of tradition, but for the Frenchmen it is more than that. Bound up in their tradition of winning the big games is the squad's French-Canadian makeup. The team plays for the Canadian province of Quebec. When it loses, the French-speaking populace is in despair. When it wins, their morale is elevated. It is almost as if the Canadiens are forever fighting a "holy war" for the honor of all Quebec's French.

A perfect example occurred in 1971, in the final game of the playoffs. The series was tied at three victories apiece between Montreal and Chicago. The final game would be played in Chicago—a distinct advantage for the Black Hawks. The Chicagoans took a 2-0 lead. But the Canadiens came back to tie the score. Then Henri Richard, a Canadien who had been benched earlier in the series, came in to play—and scored the winning goal!

High drama follows the Canadiens, even into their dressing room at the Forum. Along the walls of the room are color photographs of outstanding former Canadiens, including Maurice ("Rocket") Richard and Howie Morenz. Above the pictures is an excerpt from a World War I inspirational poem that reads: "To you from failing hands we throw the torch—be yours to hold it high." In the tense atmosphere before a game, or between periods, more than one coach has called attention to the pictures and the sentence, and inspired players to reach beyond their limits.

The Canadiens have won the Cup more times than any other club. In the National Hockey League's first 54 seasons, from the 1917 season through 1971, the Frenchmen took it 17 times. During that period they finished first a record 19 times. It is apparent from these statistics why other clubs dread facing the Montrealers in clutch games.

The Canadiens, formed in 1909, along with the National Hockey Association—the NHL's predecessor—are the only team left from that era. They were born in turbulence. Ambrose O'Brien, a millionaire railroadman from Renfrew, Ontario, had tried unsuccessfully to get his Renfrew Millionaires team into the Eastern League. Angered by the refusal, he formed his own league—the NHA. One of the new teams was the Canadiens.

O'Brien, who put up the money to start the Canadiens, was sure that a team representing Canada's French-speaking population would succeed. The French fans would finally have ice hockey players with whom they could identify.

The Canadiens didn't exactly flatten the opposition that first season. They finished last, winning two games and losing ten. Montreal's "English" team, the Wanderers, finished first. Although the situation was soon to be reversed, the two teams al-

Jean Beliveau of Montreal about to score the 500th goal of his career against North Stars, becoming first center in NHL history to reach that total.

Ken Dryden, Montreal goaltender, contends for puck with Chico Maki of Black Hawks in '71 Cup playoff game. At right is Canadiens' Guy Lapointe.

ways remained distant. The French players on the Canadiens rarely spoke to the English players on the Wanderers, and in the years to come their battles were hardly less fierce than some of the early military struggles between England and France.

The Canadiens produced one outstanding player in their inaugural season—Edouard ("Newsy") Lalonde, who got his nickname because he once worked in a newspaper plant. Lalonde was a flashy forward who used his head as much as his feet. He had also been an outstanding lacross player; in fact, some experts have indicated he was the finest lacrosse player Canada ever produced. In their second season the Canadiens acquired Georges Vezina, the goalie, who came to be known as the Chicoutimi Cucumber because of his coolness under pressure.

Vezina played in an era when goalies weren't permitted to go to the ice to make saves—they were required to stand erect. He had learned his hockey in a curious way. He didn't like ice skates—and he never wore them until he was 20 years old. The Canadiens saw him for the first time when he was 21, during an exhibition game with his Chicoutimi team. When they had not yet scored in the first period, the Canadiens figured that Vezina had been lucky. But midway through the second period, they still hadn't scored, and they became furious. The game no longer was an exhibition contest for them—they wanted to get the puck past this upstart goalie. They couldn't. He shut them out. Soon, Vezina was a Canadien himself.

From the time he put on his first pair of Canadien skates until his last game 15 years later, Georges Vezina never missed a game for the Montrealers. He started the 1925-1926 season, but his health was failing. He looked weak and had lost weight; yet he played with the same determination as always. Vezina, a gentle, pipe-smoking

man given to writing philosophical essays was in the final stages of tuberculosis. H started a game against Pittsburgh in No vember, but severe chest pains forced hin to drop out after the first period. Fou months later he was dead.

By then, the Canadiens had solidly es tablished themselves. One of the team' heroes was Joe Malone. During the 1917 1918 campaign, Malone produced 4 goals in 20 games—the only Nationa Hockey League player ever to average more than two goals a game for a season When he set this record, though, it didn' create the sensation that followed almos 30 years later—when the 44-goal tota was eclipsed by Maurice Richard. The Rocket was the first player to score 50 goals, a figure he reached during the 1944 1945 season.

"People ask me more about my 44 goal; when the Rocket broke the record than they did when I set it," Malone reflected.

Malone's teammate was Joe ("Bad Joe") Hall, a 150-pound defenseman who played the game with such abandon that opponents often were sent sprawling on the ice. With Malone, Hall and Vezina as the leaders, the Canadiens had every hope of capturing their first Cup in the NHL in 1919 (they had won one in the old NHA). They challenged Seattle. The coast team won two of the first three games. The fourth game went into an hour and forty minutes of overtime—and then was called a draw. The teams played again, and again they went into overtime. But the Canadiens got the winning goal to even the series.

Some believe that that was the beginning of the Canadiens' tradition of never giving up. But when the game was over, Hall trudged wearily off the ice. He hadn't played with his usual flair. As it turned out, Hall was a victim of the most serious flu epidemic that had ever struck Canada, and died within six days. The series was canceled because of the heavy toll the flu had taken on both clubs. It was the only time the Cup wasn't awarded after a hockey season.

The Cup eluded the Canadiens until the 1923-1924 season, when Howie Morenz joined the club. It was more than a coincidence. To this day, old-timers insist that Morenz was not only the fastest skater ice hockey has produced, but also its finest player. He was part of the Golden Age of Sports—the 1920's—and became "the Babe Ruth of Hockey." It seems difficult to believe, but before Morenz joined the Canadiens, they were hardly a national institution; virtually all of their followers were in Quebec. Morenz's style was meteoric, typified by headlong rushes that made the other team's defenders look foolish. All sorts of ways were devised to stop him. Before he joined the Canadiens, for example, a team once tried to halt him by having him arrested during a game. In scooting behind the opposition's goal, his stick had accidentally struck the goal judge in the foot, and torn the judge's rubber overshoes. Between periods, the other team arranged for a summons, which was duly presented to Morenz by a policeman "for defacing private property."

A few years later, when teams from the United States joined the league, Morenz was acknowledged as hockey's greatest gate attraction. As one of the few recognized hockey players in the States, he helped significantly in promoting popularity of the sport south of the Canadian border.

Morenz's career came to a tragic end in his fourteenth season, early in 1937, when he broke his leg in a game. He died less than two months later, following complications. Montreal went into mourning for Morenz, who had been named the league's most valuable player three times, and had averaged one goal for every two games he played. More than a hundred thousand people came to pay their last respects at his funeral, and he was accorded honors usually reserved for heads of state.

Morenz was symbolic of the Canadiens' style—fast and good. The fans of the French team were as wrapped up in the game as the players. Over the years, the Canadiens came to stand for a style of play that could best be described as "excitement."

Another member of the Morenz era was Aurel Joliat, a 135-pound flash who came to the Canadiens in a deal for Lalonde. When the trade was made in 1922, the Canadiens' followers were angered. Lalonde, after all, had taken on the stature of a folk-hero, the finest athlete the French community had produced. Joliat? A pipsqueak. But his drive soon made the fans forgive the Canadiens. Joliat's style was once compared to the finesse of a ballet dancer. He replied, "A fellow *needs* finesse when he weighs only 135 pounds." Joliat scored as many goals as Morenz— 270. He suffered more injuries than most players, though. His size made him a difficult target, but once an opponent hit him, it was disastrous. Joliat ultimately wound up his career after suffering six shoulder separations, three broken ribs, and five nose fractures.

Although Newsy Lalonde had long since been traded, his heart remained in Montreal. Even while playing for Saskatoon, Lalonde told the Canadiens' owner, Leo Dandurand, about a young goalie named George Hainsworth. "Keep him in mind, in case Vezina ever retires," Lalonde wrote.

Thus it was that Hainsworth joined the Frenchmen in 1926, shortly after Georges Venzia's death. He wasn't tall for a goalie —only five feet six—and he was already 31 years old. But in his first three seasons he captured the newly named Vezina Trophy, for permitting the fewest goals.

By the mid-1930's, the Canadian dy-

Montreal's Ralph Backstrom is jammed against boards by Chicago's Matt Ravlich.

nasty suddenly ended. The players had grown older, but management hadn't had the foresight to bring up younger talent. In 1936, the Forum management took over control of the team. It now had two hockey clubs—the Canadiens and the English-oriented Maroons. Both were losing money. The Forum decided to drop one of the clubs. Since the Canadiens had more widespread appeal, the Maroons bowed out of ice hockey.

Outstanding players continued to develop and one of the best was Hector ("Toe") Blake, who joined the Canadiens in 1935. He won the scoring title three seasons later. The Canadiens, as a team, however, were at the bottom—they finished last in 1940. Dick Irvin, dismissed by Toronto as "too old," subsequently took over as coach. During the next three campaigns the Canadiens slowly moved back toward the top. In 1942-1943, rookie Maurice ("Rocket") Richard joined the team. Elmer Lach was made Richard's center, and Blake was the left wing. The trio soon became known as the "Punch Line." But Richard broke an ankle early that first season, and was finished for the year.

In 1943, the Rocket was ready to play full-time, and under his influence the Canadiens went on to finish first and recapture the Cup. Irvin insisted the players skate, and skate fast. The style became known as "Firewagon Hockey," a name that has stuck. Richard was the engine. Not especially big, but built like a fire hydrant, he could not be legally stopped once he was near the goalie. Some extra power seemed to come from within as he charged goalward. Once, he took the puck and scored while Earl Seibert, the Hawks' defenseman, was bear-hugging him.

Along with Richard, a goalie named Bill Durnan had recently joined the team. In his first season, Durnan won the Vezina Trophy, a feat he was to achieve six times in a seven-year career.

In the 1944 playoffs, Richard began a tradition of scoring the important goals. He scored 12 in the nine playoff games, adding 9 assists for 21 points. No one is even close to his career mark of 83 winning goals. In 133 playoff games he accounted for a record 82 goals. He acquired legendary proportions quite early in his career. It was during the 1944-1945 season that he became the first player to score 50 goals in a year. During the campaign he set a record of eight points in one game— five goals and three assists. They came after a day which he had spent moving into a new house.

To make sure the Canadiens remained on top, Frank Selke joined the Canadiens in 1946 as general manager, after a successful career with Toronto. The Canadiens were in danger of becoming stale, as they had done during the 1930's. Selke quickly built up the largest farm system in hockey —the Canadiens had more players in their organization than the other five teams combined.

The Canadiens' domination continued, reaching a peak in the mid-1950's, when it was filled with the young stars that Selke had developed and Irvin had molded. Richard was still scoring goals, and his younger brother Henri, a spirited little center, had come along. Bernie ("Boom-Boom") Geoffrion and Jean Beliveau were there. Dickie Moore, who was to set a single-season point record, also starred, along with Bert Olmstead. The defense was anchored by Doug Harvey, one of the smoothest, most unflappable rear guards the sport has produced. From 1958 to 1962, the team finished first in five straight seasons.

Geoffrion had been on the team longer than Beliveau, and assumed that he would inherit the crown from Richard as No. 1 in Montreal. But then Beliveau came along and he was also a star. Geoffrion became the second man to get 50 goals when he reached the figure in the 1960-1961 season, the Canadiens' first season without the Rocket, who had retired. But it was Beliveau, not Geoffrion, who was named team captain. As though to show his teammates a thing or two, Geoffrion went out and had the finest season of his career.

There were many similarities between the Boomer and the Rocket. Each was explosively tempered, and each felt the greatest insult possible was to be deprived of a goal. Both were moody and intense, and when they fought, they fought viciously. Beliveau, on the other hand, was at first content to play an easygoing game, taking hostile sticks and elbows in stride. He soon learned that being a nice guy didn't pay dividends, and he retaliated. As his penalty minutes grew, so did his goal output.

The Canadiens' goalie during this great era was Jacques Plante, more popular with fans and writers than with his own teammates. Plante produced some of the finest goaltending ever seen, but when he lost, or allowed a goal, he invariably would blame it on the team. Plante also was a hypochondriac, given to asthmatic spells. He used to claim he was allergic to Toronto. Some of his teammates believed he was allergic to the Toronto shooters. Hector ("Toe") Blake, who replaced Dick Irvin as coach in 1955, had mixed feelings about Plante. His goalie always seemed to be complaining. But there was no doubt that he produced. Blake was opposed to a Plante idea that was to revolutionize goaltending—the mask. The goalie had been in action against the Rangers in New York, had got sliced in the face with a puck, and was stitched up. Between periods, he told Blake he wanted to wear a mask. "Go ahead, if you want to," growled Blake reluctantly, knowing that Plante wouldn't continue without one. Plante put it on—and never took it off. He was the first goalie to wear the mask regularly, and now virtually every netminder considers i a piece of necessary equipment.

Blake ended his 13-year coaching reig in 1968, after the Frenchmen had cap tured their eighth Cup, and had finishe first nine times, under his guidance. Sam Pollock, the astute general manager of th Canadiens, and regarded as the best front office man in hockey, selected Claud Ruel to replace Blake. Ruel was unknow outside the Canadiens' organization, an was only 30 years old when appointed— the youngest coach in the NHL. "I have t repeat," said Ruel. "If I don't, everyon will say I'm responsible. I can't win. If th club finishes first, they'll say it was becaus I took over a winner. If I lose, they'll sa I had a winner and couldn't repeat." Bu Ruel repeated, using such old-timers a Jean Beliveau and Henri Richard. Th other stars had gone, but there were som good players in Jacques Lemaire, Serg Savard, Bobby Rousseau, Yvan Cournoy er, John Ferguson, and Lorne ("Gump" Worsley in goal. Ferguson was the tough est of the Canadiens, who were more con cerned with skating and scoring than figh ing. Ferguson was their "policeman." Wor sley, a tubby man who always had weight problem, confounded fans with hi acrobatics.

But old age had at last caught up witl them. The Canadiens struggled throug the 1969-1970 season, and whether the made the playoffs was dependent on wha they did in their final game against Chi cago. The first four teams in each divisio qualified for the Cup games. The Canadi ens entered their last game tied in point with the Rangers for fourth place. All th Canadiens needed was a tie to gain on point and take over fourth. The Ranger had finished the season that afternoon witl an astonishing 9-5 victory over the Re Wings. The goal outburst gave the Nev Yorkers a season goal-total of 246. Th

Ted Harris of Canadiens goes flying as Boston's Derek Sanderson (left) and Don Awrey (right) block him off.

(Wide World)

Canadiens had 242. Even if the Canadiens lost, they could still make the playoffs if they had more than 246 goals.

The Canadiens were routed, 10-2. Their dynasty was ended. They had failed to make the playoffs after a record twenty-one straight seasons of Cup play. The Canadiens began the 1970-1971 season with some new faces. After a few games, Ruel was fired and Al MacNeil, a former defenseman, took over. Then the Canadiens acquired one of the league's scoring stars, Frank Mahovlich, from Detroit. Frank's brother, Pete, blossomed as a goal-scorer. Jean Beliveau was rejuvenated. Once again the Canadiens moved. They finished third. In the playoffs, they called on a rookie goalie from Cornell University, Ken Dryden, to man the nets. They upset the Boston Bruins, who had finished with the greatest goal-scoring record and the most points, in a seven-game Cup series. Then they got by the Minnesota North Stars in six games of the second round. They faced the Hawks for the Stanley Cup, and won it on Richard's goal in the seventh game. Dryden was named the outstanding player in the playoffs. Shortly after, Beliveau and Ferguson announced their retirement. Only Henri Richard remained as

a link with the past. But the Canadiens were ready to start a new dynasty. They hired Scotty Bowman, the man who had virtually created the expansion St. Louis Blues, as coach to replace MacNeil. In the draft, they acquired Guy Lafleur, considered Canada's best amateur. They appeared to be moving toward the top again.

In 1971-1972, Dryden did an unusual thing. Technically, he was still a rookie, yet he appeared in more games (64) than any other goalie and turned in eight shutouts. He won the rookie-of-the-year award and became the first player ever to win a rookie award the season after he had captured an award as the playoffs' top performer.

Pollock's transformation of the club was nearly complete. It finished third again, behind powerful Boston and Ranger teams. But it had a host of stars in Dryden, the Mahovlich Brothers, Cournoyer, and Jacques Lemaire, to complement outstanding defensemen. And even more important, Pollock had planned for the future—he had an exciting bunch of youngsters waiting in the wings. They matured early and gave the Frenchmen another first-place finish in 1972-1973, as the club lost only 10 games, a record.

New York Rangers

From 1943 to 1966, as many fans will still remember, the Rangers missed the playoffs 18 times. They finished as high as second only once. They had some of the worst, funniest, most outrageous teams in the sport's history. During their long period of incompetence, they were compared to the old Brooklyn Dodgers, baseball's famous losers of the 1930's. Ironically, the Rangers' worst period began the season after they finished first. The bottom fell out after the 1941-1942 campaign, when virtually the entire team left to join the armed forces. The club finished last for four straight seasons, and it would not recover fully until 1967.

The atmosphere in New York, strangely, was negative for hockey players. Baseball, football and basketball players welcomed the prospect of playing in the big city, where the big salaries were. It was easier to become famous in New York, the home of the major magazines, newspapers, and radio and television networks. Players in New York got more exposure than did players in other cities. But hockey players always preferred to play in Canada. New York somehow seemed alien. And when the team was a loser, with poor traveling conditions and skimpy meal allowances and dwindling numbers of fans—well, it became an impossible situation for Canadian players. At least, if they were going to be laughed at, they would rather be laughingstocks back home.

Yet, when the Rangers started in 1926, they were not only the best of the new teams, but the best in the entire NHL. The success of the Americans in Madison Square Garden the previous year spurred a search for another New York team to play in the new arena, which needed attractions to pay the mortgage. Tex Rickard (a Midwesterner who had adopted Texas as his

home) was the Garden's head. He was skeptical about ice hockey when the Americans joined the league, but after a few months he became aware of its enormous financial potential. The Garden didn't own the Americans—it merely rented the building to them. Rickard wanted a club of his own whose profits he could keep.

One of his advisors was Colonel John S. Hammond, a former military attaché in Argentina, whose knowledge of hockey was limited. But Hammond had heard of a young man in Toronto named Conn Smythe, who was highly successful in developing local amateur teams in Canada. Colonel Hammond was named the president of a new team, which would be called the Rangers, since Rickard had a fondness for the exploits of the heroes of the old West. Hammond immediately hired Smythe as coach and general manager of the club. Smythe laid the groundwork, acquiring many name players, but as soon as training

In memorable performance, Ranger Coach Frank Boucher, retired as a player for many years, returns to action in November 7, 1943 game at Madison Square Garden and scores despite efforts of Chicago's Virg Johnson and goalie Hec Higton.

(UPI)

began, he was suddenly dismissed. (Smythe claimed later that Hammond, unsure of himself, was talked into hiring a man with a proven reputation.) The replacement was Lester Patrick.

Patrick had sold his league out west, and was seeking a new career. His name had already taken on legendary proportions through the hockey world. Luckily, some of the players from his old league followed him to the Rangers. The New Yorkers that first year included three who made the Hall of Fame. The big defenseman for the team was Ching Johnson, a brawler who was one of the most pugnacious players in the Rangers' Golden Era. Frank Boucher, a diminutive center who remained with the Ranger organization for 30 years, was another. There were also the Cook Brothers, Bill and Bun. Bill, the better player of the two,

led the league in goals with 33 in his first season.

With this talent, the Rangers finished first in their first year, with an 11-point margin over the second-place Bruins. It was perhaps the first time in modern sports history that a new entrant finished atop the league standings.

The Rangers traded places with the Bruins in their second season (1927-1928), but went on to win the Stanley Cup with one of those amazing storybook achievements exhibited now and then in the world of sports. The Rangers got past Pittsburgh in the first round, and then eliminated the tough Bruins in the semi-finals. They faced the Montreal Maroons for the Cup. But the Rangers couldn't play their finals in Madison Square Garden, because the arena was booked for other events. All games would have to take place at the Forum in Montreal. Thus, the New Yorkers wouldn't have the benefit of home ice in their contest against a power-packed Maroon lineup. The Montreal stars included Nels Stewart, Babe Siebert and Hooley Smith.

The Rangers were in deep trouble after the opening game—they lost, 2-0. The first club to win three games would capture the Cup. Still, the Rangers were confident as they took to the ice for Game No. 2. Their goalie, Lorne Chabot, had done a good job against the powerful Maroons. If the Rangers could get some scoring, Patrick believed, they could win. Chabot again played well, and midway through the second period neither team had scored. Then a shot by Stewart hit Chabot in the left eye, and the goalie went to the dressing room for treatment. The entire Ranger team accompanied him as an intermission was called. With no two-goalie system in those days, when a goaltender was injured, play was halted until he could return. The doctor, however, told Patrick that Chabot couldn't continue play. It wasn't unusual for the home team to have a spare goalie sitting in the stands, ready for duty with either team in case of an injury. That night, however, the Maroons didn't have anyone in the stands. But there were two goalies from other clubs—Alex Connell of Ottawa, and Hughie McCormick, a minor-leaguer. Patrick left the dressing room and asked Eddie Gerard, the Maroons' general manager, if the Rangers could use either Connell or McCormick. Gerard stuck to the rules and refused to permit either man to play for New York.

Patrick went back to the dressing room, faced with one of his most difficult problems. No other player on the team thought he could handle the goaltending duties.

All eyes turned to Patrick, wondering what he'd do. At 44, Patrick's hair had already turned white, earning him the nickname of "The Silver Fox." He was still lean of body, and had kept himself in shape. Suddenly, Patrick announced: "I'm going to play goal, fellows." The players were stunned. They knew he had once been a great defenseman—but he hadn't played in 14 years. Patrick advised his players, before putting on the pads, "Check as you've never checked before—and help protect an old man!"

Patrick's dramatic decision did wonders for the Rangers. They stormed onto the ice and pressured the Maroons. If any Montreal player even approached the "old man" in goal, a Ranger would send the intruder sprawling. It seemed impossible, but the Rangers were containing the Maroons. Early in the final period, the bizarre game turned—Bill Cook scored, and the Rangers gained a 1-0 lead. The impossible was happening. But Nels Stewart continued to hound the Rangers. With the game almost over, he scored for the Maroons—and forced the contest into overtime. It was sudden death, with the winner being the team that scored first. Frank Boucher scored, and the Rangers won. It seemed almost anti-climactic that the Rangers won the Cup. They found a goalie named Joe Miller, who filled in for Chabot. In the final game, Boucher scored twice and the New Yorkers had their championship. It was the first of only three Cups the Rangers captured in their first 45 years.

Frank Boucher was one of the Rangers' dominant figures. He centered for the Cook boys, and enjoyed a reputation as one of the cleanest players in the game. Indeed, he won the Lady Byng Trophy—awarded for clean play coupled with skill—for four straight seasons, and seven times in eight years. He was so highly regarded that after he took it for the seventh time, the league presented him with the trophy as a permanent possession.

The Cook boys and Boucher brought the Rangers another first-place finish during the 1931-1932 season, and another Cup in 1933. But the team was now seven years old, and age was beginning to show. Although the players were still solid contenders, Patrick decided it was time to bring in some new blood. In the mid-1930's, the Patrick farm system paid off. Promising youngsters joined the big club, including Bryan Hextall, Phil Watson, Alex Shibicky and Patrick's own sons, Lynn and Muzz. It was a rollicking team that had a good deal of fun. There were times when the Rangers were the primary sports attraction in New York City, as fans turned out to see this happy-go-lucky collection. They were joined by Davey Kerr, who was to become a top goalie.

Patrick had been the coach and general manager since the team began. After the 1938-1939 season, he turned the coaching over to Frank Boucher, who had retired as a player. When Boucher took over, he immediately began to test some radical concepts of his own, one of them being the "box defense," in which the Rangers formed a rectangle when one of their men was in the penalty box and they were a man short. They stationed themselves on their side of the ice in the box position, and it enabled them to protect all corners.

Perhaps Boucher's most interesting idea was in replacing the goalie. All teams today take a goalie out in the final minute of play when they are trailing by a goal, the idea being to gain an extra attacker and attempt to tie the score. Before Boucher came along, some teams did take their goalie out, but only when there was a face-off on the other side of the ice. The opposition was able to prepare for the change, since it took place at the beginning of a new period, when the players faced the puck. Boucher believed he could make the shift while play was in progress—he would sud-

(UPI)

Murray Patrick tallies deciding Ranger goal in fourth game of '39 Stanley Cup playoffs for 2–1 victory over Bruins.

denly signal his goalie to leave, and place an extra forward on the ice during the actual play. All he needed was an opportunity to test the procedure.

The Rangers were so good under Boucher in his first season that they rarely trailed in a game. In fact, while Boucher was hoping to test his theory, the New Yorkers played a 19-game stretch in which they went undefeated—14 victories and five ties. In the twentieth game, they were playing the Black Hawks at Chicago and trailed by 1-0 in the final seconds. The time was

Puck, shot by Rangers' Don Marshall, scoots under Chicago's Glenn Hall and into net. Camera was placed inside goal and operated by remote control.

Ed Giacomin of Rangers imitates Jackie Gleason's away-we-go motion while making save against Canadiens.

ripe for Boucher's innovational plan. The play was going strong in the Hawks' end, and Boucher signaled for Kerr to leave the ice. Patrick was sitting on the bench. He hadn't been told about Boucher's strategy. As he watched the action, he saw one of the Rangers suddenly leap over the sideboards and skate onto the ice. Patrick didn't realize that Kerr was coming off, and he shouted to the new Ranger on the ice to come back to the bench, mistakenly concluding that there were too many men on the ice, which called for a penalty.

When the referee heard Patrick shouting, he halted play. Then he told Boucher he was penalizing the Rangers for having an extra man in play. Boucher explained that the Rangers had the legal number of six men. By then it was too late. The Rangers' momentum was stopped, and Chicago won, halting the Rangers' streak. The Rangers won their next five games, for a record of only one loss in 25 games —more than half the season.

In early 1940, at the end of Boucher's first year, the Rangers won the Cup—the only Cup they would win through the 1940's, 1950's and 1960's. The Rangers were so good that year that they won, even though forced to play the Cup final against the Maple Leafs at Toronto—once again, Madison Square Garden in New York was unavailable. Three of the final games ended in ties, and the Rangers won all the overtime contests. It appeared to be the beginning of an outstanding era, perhaps a dynasty. The Rangers were good and young, with such stars as Neil and Mac Colville and Art Coulter starring along with the other proven players. By the end of the 1941-1942 season, the Rangers had finished first again. There were only bright prospects ahead.

But World War II was in progress, and the Rangers lost more than half their starters to the armed services. They fell from first to last place, and stayed there for four straight seasons. The long drought was under way. They set a record by failing to win for 25 straight games, and also absorbed the worst defeat of modern ice hockey—a 15-0 loss to the Red Wings. During the 1943-1944 season, they compiled one of the poorest records in history by winning only six of 50 games. Frank Boucher, at 42, was forced to come out of retirement in a vain effort to help his foundering club.

When the war ended and the Rangers had again finished last, Patrick was replaced. Boucher took over as general manager in 1946, and ended Patrick's 20-year association with the Rangers. During the last trying years, the Rangers had turned from stars into clowns, and nothing was left for their fans except occasional glimpses of humor. Phil Watson, a French Canadian with limited use of English, once screamed at an opponent who had hit him: "You're nothing but a been-has!"

The fans had hopes for a brighter day when the Rangers hired a psychologist to give them a winning attitude. The doctor entered the dressing room before a game with the Boston Bruins. He tried to "psyche" the players into believing they were all-powerful, and that nobody could stop them if they only believed they were good. The Rangers did fairly well in the game. They were holding the Bruins to a tie. But late in the contest a long shot hopped past the goalie, Chuck Rayner, and the spell was broken.

Wholesale changes of players and coaches became the rule. Nevertheless, there were several good players of the late 1940's and early 1950's, including Rayner, Edgar Laprade, Tony Leswick and Allan Stanley. But it seemed that a pattern of losing had been established, and the Rangers just couldn't break out of it. Young stars, though, were developing in the minors, and in the early 1950's, before Boucher stepped down as general manager, the Rangers brought up Andy Bathgate, Harry Howell, Lou Fontinato and Dean Prentice, among others. With the fiery Watson as the coach and Muzz Patrick as general manager, the Rangers made the playoffs in three straight seasons. In each playoff, though, they were eliminated in the first round. During the 1958-1959 campaign, it appeared the Rangers would again make the playoffs. They were comfortably in fourth place (the last playoff berth), with a huge lead over Toronto.

In fact, the only way they could lose was to fail to win any of their remaining games, while the Maple Leafs had to win all their final games. But that's exactly what happened! The Rangers managed just one tie during the last two weeks, and dropped to fifth. Another pattern had been established: the Rangers couldn't win the big games. They choked.

They had a brief fling with the playoffs again during the 1961-1962 season, when the great Doug Harvey was traded to the Rangers from Montreal. Harvey was the player-coach, and his coolness under fire led the Rangers back into fourth place. Once more, the Rangers folded in the first round of Cup play. Despite the presence of Bathgate, one of the true superstars, most of the Rangers were too small. One of their leading scorers was Camille Henry, who was only five feet eight, and weighed 140. The Rangers were pushed around.

More changes were made, with the hope that the New Yorkers could acquire youth and muscle. Finally, Muzz Patrick was ousted as general manager, and his assistant, Emile Francis, a former goalie Muzz had brought into the organization, replaced him. Francis also took over the coaching duties, and when the 1966-1967 season began, the Rangers were in Francis's hands. He was on top of an organiza-

tion that he had radically altered, and his first order of business was building a team that could get into the playoffs.

One of his projects was Ed Giacomin, a grayish goalie who had come up the season before, but was an inconsistent player. Giacomin was known as a wanderer. Unlike most other goalies, he often left his cage to halt the enemy.

When the 1966-1967 season began, Francis wasn't sure whether Giacomin or Cesare Maniago would be his regular goalie. Maniago was more dependable. But late in the first period of a game, Maniago got hit in the mouth by a puck. He went to the bench for repairs, and came back to finish the period. During the intermission Maniago told Francis he was unable to continue. Maniago had broken an unwritten rule of hockey: if you're well enough to walk to the bench, you're well enough to play. Giacomin replaced Maniago for the rest of the game. At the next day's practice, Francis told Giacomin: "You're my goalie from now on."

As significant as Giacomin's coming of age was the "unretirement" of Bernie ("Boom-Boom") Geoffrion. The Boomer had been retired for two years, but Francis persuaded him to come back. Geoffrion immediately infused the Rangers with the Montreal spirit. He convinced them they could be a contender "if you think you are."

Geoffrion's constant prodding made believers of such young Rangers as Rod Gilbert, Jean Ratelle, Vic Hadfield, Jim Neilson, Arnie Brown, Rod Seiling and Bob Nevin. The Rangers, who had been out of the playoffs for four straight seasons, suddenly were near the top of the league. For half the season they were first or second, but then they went into a tailspin. They did make the playoffs, though, finishing fourth. But their reputation for not winning the big ones remained with them. In the first game of their playoff series with Montreal, they were leading by 4-1 late in the third period. They lost the game, 6-4, and went down to defeat in four straight contests.

It was during the 1967-1968 season that the Rangers arrived. A solid team, they made it to second place. Ed Giacomin, who had led the league in shutouts the season before, continued to star. The Rangers didn't have much scoring punch, though, and relied on a solid defensive style and goaltending to bring them victories. They had one player who might have scored for them, but Francis was unable to bring out his best qualities. That player was Red Berenson. Berenson was traded to the St. Louis Blues early in the season for veteran Ron Stewart; and as soon as he hit St. Louis, Berenson became a star. The Rangers continued to do poorly in the playoffs, and bowed to the Black Hawks.

Geoffrion, halted by ulcer trouble, was named coach when the 1968-1969 season began. But the Boomer wasn't suited to the coaching ranks. He never could accept defeat. When he was playing for the Rangers, his references to the Canadiens stimulated the New Yorkers. But when he coached the Rangers and they lost, he would say, "No one ever did that to us at Montreal." He lost his grip on the club and himself, and his ulcer trouble flared up. By mid-season he collapsed and was hospitalized, and Francis again took over the coaching reins with the team in last place. Francis did a remarkable job, and the Rangers finished third. But they faced the Canadiens in the first round of playoffs, and again the Rangers dropped four in a row. The reputation of Giacomin as a playoff goalie was tarnished. He always looked better during the regular season than he did in the significant playoff contests.

That season the Rangers unveiled two new stars, both rookies: Brad Park, a defenseman, and Walt Tkaczuk, a gritty center. Both blossomed under Francis's handling. When the 1969-1970 season began, some experts picked the Rangers to go all the way to the top for the first time since 1942. And the Rangers looked as if they would, for they led the league for the first half of the season. Then injuries struck —Neilson, Park, Hadfield and Brown were sidelined. Tkaczuk, one of the league's scoring stars, slumped. So did everyone else. Somehow, the Rangers went into the final day of the season in fifth place. They played the Red Wings in the afternoon. A victory would tie them with the fourth-place Canadiens in total points. But the Rangers also had to score at least five goals, since fourth would go to the team with more goals if the clubs were tied in points.

One of the strangest scenes in hockey history unfolded that afternoon at Madison Square Garden. The Rangers got their five goals—and more. With one of the most powerful attacks of the year the Rangers won, 9-5. They had a four-goal lead over the Canadiens, who were playing the Hawks at night. If Montreal won, or even tied, then Montreal would get in. But if Chicago won, Montreal needed five goals to pass the Rangers and get into the playoffs. The Canadiens lost, 10-2, and the Rangers made the playoffs again.

Throughout the season, the Bruins had been the Rangers' nemesis. Repeatedly, they manhandled the New Yorkers. Derek Sanderson, especially, had enjoyed fighting with them. Now the Rangers faced the Bruins in the playoffs. The Rangers did just as poorly as ever in the first two games at Boston, where the Bruins beat them up. When the series resumed in New York, the fans strung banners around the Garden, calling for Boston blood.

"Kill Derek!" screamed one sign. Another proclaimed, "Don't Talk to the Animals —Kill Them!" Goaded on by hysterical fans, the Rangers fought back and a dirty game unfolded. By the end of the first period, Dave Balon and Derek Sanderson had been ejected. Some unruly spectators had halted play for 20 minutes by tossing eggs and balls and rubber chickens on the ice. In the end the Rangers won the game, but only after both teams had played the most penalty-filled game in the 77-year history of the playoffs—a total of 174 minutes in penalties were handed out. The playoffs were quieter after that. The Bruins went on to win, and once again the Ranger reputa-

tion as poor playoff-performers continued.

It changed in 1971. By finishing second, the Rangers had made the playoffs for five straight years, a feat they had not accomplished since 1942. They used a two-goalie system, Eddie Giacomin alternating with Gilles Villemure, and captured the Vezina Trophy. It was a well-balanced club. It proved it in the playoffs. For the first time since 1950 it got past the first round, defeating the Maple Leafs. But in the semifinals, the Rangers bowed to the Black

Hawks. Still, the New Yorkers had finally showed they were capable of winning the big games.

They proved it again in 1972 when, for the first time since 1950, they got to the final round. They bowed in six games to Boston, whose Gerry Cheevers performed remarkably in goal. Yet the Rangers had to play without Jean Ratelle, who had blossomed into one of the league's stars. So had Gilbert and Hadfield. The trio became the first line on which each member amassed at least 40 goals. They probably would have set a record for most points by a line in a season if Ratelle had not broken his ankle during the last month of the campaign. The Rangers, though, had turned into an efficient machine filled with interchangeable parts. Under Francis's masterful direction, the club was able to overcome injuries so well that they were the envy of the rest of the league.

Rangers' Dale Rolfe pokes his stick between legs of Kings' Lucien Grenier. (Wide World)

Toronto Maple Leafs

Winning in the clutch—that has been the Leafs' reputation. It has been earned. For Conn Smythe, the man who led the Torontonians through most of their great years, the "clutch" meant the Stanley Cup. He often admitted that finishing first during the regular season was nice, but winning the Cup was even more important. So he surrounded himself with players who could come up with star performances, even if it was only for a short span of time. He didn't mind resting his stars late in the season—though it might mean the Leafs' losing a hold on first place or second place—as long as it kept his team fresh for the Stanley Cup.

There was logic in the theory. Through 1972, the Leafs had captured the Cup 13 times, a record surpassed only by the Canadiens' 16 triumphs. But the Canadiens had finished first 19 times, while the Leafs had taken first only seven times. Over that span, Detroit finished first 13 times, but won only seven Cups, and the Bruins finished first 10 times, but took the Cup only on four occasions. Thus, the Leafs won the Cup repeatedly when they didn't have the "best" team, merely the "clutch" team. They are the only team to have won the Cup more often than finishing first.

The Leafs have the distinction of winning the first Cup in the National Hockey League. The triumph came following the league's formation for the 1917-1918 season. The Toronto franchise then was known as the Arenas. Ironically, a deteriorating situation in Toronto had led to the formation of the NHL. The league had been unhappy with the Arenas' owner, Eddie Livingstone, and changed its name from the National Hockey Association, enabling it to form a new corporation and kicking out Livingstone.

Supposedly, Livingstone stepped down and the new owners took over. That was the only way Toronto could join the NHL. Charles Querrie, a sportswriter and former lacrosse star, became the team's manager, and immediately set out to show who was boss. He posted a set of six rules in the dressing room, the first of which read: "First and foremost, do not forget I am running this club."

But after a few weeks, Querrie suddenly resigned—he contended that Livingstone was interfering. It was obvious that Livingstone had kept a firm hand, probably as a silent partner, in the club's fortunes. Querrie was soon persuaded to return to the job with assurances that he would receive no more second-guessing from Livingstone. The Arenas finished second to the Canadiens the first half of the season, a notable accomplishment, considering all the front-office bickering. They won the second half title, though, led by a new Querrie acquisition, goalie Harry Holmes.

The two teams that were to dominate Stanley Cup play—the Canadiens and the Toronto entry—faced each other for the right to play the Pacific Coast league for the Cup. It was a two-game playoff, and the Maple Leafs trounced the Canadiens in the opener by 7-3. Whether by luck or design, Newsy Lalonde spent so much time fighting with Toronto players that he was rarely in scoring position, though he managed to score twice. In the second game, Lalonde again scored twice, as the Canadiens won, 4-3. But Toronto captured the playoff on the basis of goals scored. They faced Vancouver for the Cup, with the honor of the NHL in the balance. The previous year the Seattle Metropolitans had won the Cup. Toronto was determined to return the Cup to the East.

The final playoffs were to be played alternately with eastern and western rules. The chief difference was in the forward-passing zone that the Patricks had devised.

Garry Monahan, Maple Leafs' left wing, takes control of puck as Jean Guy Lagace of Penguins gets face full of ice in '73 game at Pittsburgh.

Toronto's Brian Conacher looks as if he has taken a right to the jaw from
Ed Van Impe of Black Hawks as goaltender Denis DeJordy blocks his shot.

(UPI)

Toronto won the first game, under eastern rules, and Vancouver won the second under western rules. The situation remained the same through the third and fourth games. In the deciding game, the Arenas had the advantage of their eastern rules. They captured the final game, 2-1—and had the first Cup the new NHL won. One of their stars was Alf Skinner, who began the Toronto tradition of playing better in the Cup games than in the regular season. Skinner scored eight goals in seven play-off contests—compared to 13 goals during 19 regular-season games. Perhaps the most extraordinary aspect of Toronto's victory was this: it marked the last time anyone other than NHL teams competed for the Cup.

Curiously, the Arenas had a young player named Jack Adams, who had just turned pro, but failed to score in eight regular-season games. During the 1918-1919 season, he was just as unspectacular—and was traded to Vancouver, where he eventually blossomed into stardom. As the 1919-1920 season began, there were other changes in the Toronto team—including the name, which was changed from the Arenas to the St. Patricks.

That season, a smallish forward named Cecil Henry ("Babe") Dye joined the St. Pats. At five feet eight and 150 pounds, Dye had trouble cracking the starting line-up. He got into parts of 21 games, and scored 11 goals.

But because he was so small, the Toronto management didn't think he could help the club. In Dye's second season, the Quebec franchise was moved to Hamilton. The fans in Hamilton weren't anxious to turn out to see a bad hockey club, and the other teams in the league were requested to provide Hamilton with good players to help attendance. The St. Pats provided Dye. After one game they changed their mind, took back Dye, and provided another player. It was a fortunate move. Dye went on to lead the league in scoring, with the astounding total of 35 goals in only 24 games. The Leafs finished first. In 1922, the Leafs again won the Cup, with Dye scoring nine goals in the five-game final against Vancouver.

Dye's scoring percentage was the second-highest of any man who ever performed in the NHL. In his six seasons following his rookie year, he scored 163 goals in 149 games. He led the league in scoring four times and twice scored five goals in a game. Dye accomplished this in only nine seasons. He moved to Chicago in 1926 when the league expanded, but he broke a leg during training in 1927, and sat out most of that season. He gave it one more try, with the New York Americans in 1928-1929, and scored only once in 41 games. That lowered his average. But it enabled him to reach the 200-goal club. He wound up with a scoring record of 200 goals in 271 games—a percentage of .738. Only one other player, Cyril ("Cy") Denneny of Ottawa and Boston, ever exceeded the .600 plateau (with .767).

Had Dye not been such a braggart, he probably would never have been traded to Chicago. But after an 18-goal season he went, following complaints from teammates that he was constantly telling them how good he was.

Yet, Dye was indirectly responsible for the Leafs' ultimately becoming one of the sport's powerhouses. It was because of Dye that Conn Smythe joined Toronto. When the Rangers hired Smythe in 1926 to form a team, Smythe insisted on getting young players to build a foundation. Colonel John Hammond, the Ranger's president, wanted Smythe to acquire Dye. But Smythe wasn't interested in the 28-year-old Dye, and went to a football game instead of making a deal with Toronto. Chicago got Dye, and Hammond, furious, immediately fired Smythe

—before the Rangers had even played a game.

Smythe was only 31 years old, but had a reputation as a shrewd businessman and a brilliant judge of hockey talent. He had a burning desire to remain in professional hockey—most of his adult life had been devoted to the amateur ranks. He knew that professional hockey was the wave of the future, but he didn't have the money to invest in a club. Then Smythe got lucky. He received $2,500 from Tex Rickard, the Madison Square Garden president, as a final payment on Smythe's short-lived contract with the Rangers. Smythe bet the whole sum on a college football game and won. Now he had $5,000. The Rangers were coming to Toronto to play the St. Pats, and the St. Pats were an overwhelming 3-1 favorite, since no one there believed the fledgling Ranger team could compete seriously with the established home-town squad. Smythe knew, however, that the Rangers were a good club—he had, after all, put it together. He bet the $5,000 on the Rangers—and won again. Now he had $15,000.

At the same time, Frank Selke, a union executive and longtime hockey partner of Smythe's, learned that the St. Patricks were for sale. Selke brought Smythe together with several other businessmen, and they pooled their resources. The St. Pats were available for $135,000, and Smythe's group bought them. Smythe, a zealous believer in Canada's destiny, changed the club's name to the patriotic-sounding Maple Leafs, the maple leaf being the national symbol of Canada. The Maple Leafs did not have a memorable start that first season—they finished last in the Canadian division, and lost more than $100,000.

The next season Smythe took total control. He was already the president and general manager. He also appointed himself coach. Although Smythe and Selke were recognized as two of the most knowledge-able men in the game, they failed to bring much cheer to their fans. In 1930, Smythe made three far-reaching decisions: he stepped down as coach, he acquired King Clancy, and he decided to build a new arena.

Art Duncan took over as coach, and was expected to produce. There was no room for emotionalism on the Leafs under Smythe; performance was all that mattered. Duncan was moved to the coaching ranks from defense because of the major deal that brought Clancy to Toronto. Luckily for Smythe, Ottawa was losing money and was desperate for cash. Clancy already was established as one of the top defensemen in the game, although he stood only five feet seven and weighed but 155 pounds. But Smythe gave Ottawa $35,000, and Clancy and two other players joined the Leafs.

Clancy immediately became the team leader, a raucous individual not afraid to fight or scream or get himself beaten up if he thought it could help his club. In his first season, the Leafs made second place. In his second campaign, they won the Cup. Clancy was as colorful as any player who ever put on skates. He once was beaten up by a Maroon player named Harold Starr. As Starr sat on him, he looked down at Clancy and said, "Well, I got you good this time, didn't I?" Clancy, bleeding but still pugnacious, said through broken teeth, "You never saw the day you could lay a hand on me." Over the years Clancy lost most of his teeth. Before one game he complained, "I've only got one tooth in my head—and that's the one that's hurting me." On another occasion he was ready to take to the ice when he realized he had left his St. Christopher medal at home. He got dressed, went back for it, and returned to play.

Within a few months after Clancy joined the club, the Leafs became a big drawing card. Smythe realized he had a moneymaker in the team, and early in 1931 Smythe formulated plans for a new, larger arena. The business community was skeptical. Canada was suffering through the worldwide depression that had begun in 1929, and money was unavailable. However, Selke, a shrewd if unimposing-looking businessman, came up with an alternative; why not compensate the construction workers with shares of stock in the new arena instead of cash? Hundreds of skilled Toronto laborers were out of work. Selke, through his contacts, approached union executives, who endorsed the idea. In the spring of 1931, the arena began to take shape.

The 1931-1932 season was hardly under way when Smythe made another major move. He persuaded Dick Irvin to quit as the Chicago coach and move to Toronto. Irvin relieved Art Duncan. Irvin was a serious fellow who believed in moderation. So did Smythe and Selke. Clarence ("Hap") Day, another nonsmoker and nondrinker, was appointed the team's captain. Although Smythe was to permit a few "bad actors" on his clubs through the following decades, he preferred the Spartan type of player. Day teamed on defense with King Clancy, giving the Leafs one of the finest defensive pairs in the history of the game.

It was a good year for Toronto. The rink opened in November, 1931, just about six months after ground-breaking had started, and became an immediate success. It was considered prestigious to go to a Maple Leaf game, and the arena prospered in the midst of the depression. The ultimate triumph came when the Leafs won the Cup, the first under their new name.

The heart of their scoring for most of the 1930's was the "Kid Line." Joe Primeau was the center, Harvey ("Busher") Jackson the left wing, and Charlie Conacher the right wing. The trio's scoring enabled the Maple Leafs to finish first for three straight years after the Cup victory, and four times in the next six seasons.

Jackson was an All-Star five times, although he had a problem with alcohol. He led the league in scoring once, and totaled 241 career goals. Yet, old-timers remember him panhandling outside the old Madison Square Garden after he joined the New York Americans toward the end of his career. He died in 1966. Because of his tainted image, he was denied entrance to the Hockey Hall of Fame until 1971.

Injuries plagued Charlie Conacher, who rarely managed to complete a full season. But he led the league in goal-scoring five times, and made the All-Star team five straight years. He had a career average of one goal for every two games.

Joe Primeau never received the adulation that was bestowed on his line-mates, but it was largely because of his steady play-making and unselfishness with the puck that the Maple Leafs blossomed into league-leading scorers. Primeau was an especially clean player; when the Rangers' Frank Boucher won the Lady Byng Trophy seven times in eight years, the man who beat him out that one season was Primeau. He finished second in scoring twice—once to Jackson and the other time to Conacher.

By the late 1930's, Smythe's Dynasty was nearing an end. The "Kid Line" had been broken up, and Clancy had gone. Despite the outstanding stars, four first-place finishes and three second-place finishes, the Maple Leafs captured only one Cup during the decade. Smythe methodically gave the Leafs a complete overhaul. In 1940, he appointed Hap Day as coach and dismissed Irvin. He had some new players in C. J. S. ("Syl") Apps, W. ("Turk") Broda, Gordie Drillon, and Wally Stanowski. Smythe learned that youth was the key. Said Smythe, "New players mean new blood, and they're hungrier for a Stanley Cup."

Toronto's Jacques Plante stops puck with right skate to thwart scoring bid by Phil Roberto of Blues (right) as Jim Dorey of Maple Leafs moves in.

Under Day, the Leafs became recognized as the clutch team in the playoffs. In Day's second year, 1942, the Leafs faced the Red Wings for the Cup. They dropped the first three games—but came back to win. It was the first time a club had rallied from such a deficit to take the Cup. The Leafs finished first only once during Day's ten years, but took five Stanley Cups. In 1947, they began a three-year string of Cup victories, the first club to accomplish that feat.

The new "Kid Line" included Ted Kennedy, Vic Lynn and Howie Meeker. None of these players was considered in the same class with their predecessors of the 1930's, but they worked well together, and brought Toronto success after dazzling success. Goalie Turk Broda was better in the tense playoffs than he was in the regular season. He established a record of 13 playoff shutouts in 101 appearances, and had a remarkable goals-against average of 2.08 in Cup play.

Also in this aggregation was "Wild Bill" Ezinicki, who hit everyone in an opposing team's uniform. He once struck the Rangers' Edgar Laprade so hard that Laprade suffered a concussion after falling to the ice. The Ranger coach, Frank Boucher, thereupon sent a telegram to the league president, Clarence Campbell, insisting that "a curb must be put on this player immediately." Smythe remarked, "Boucher doesn't like to see this kind of legal contact. It might give his players bad habits."

Probably the finest club of the era was the 1947-1948 squad. It finished first, Broda won the Vezina Trophy, and the club won the Cup. Syl Apps also retired. He went into the final game of the regular season with 198 career goals, and then got his two to make it an even 200 for his career.

The 1950's produced only one Cup and only one second-place finish. Except for Harry Lumley in goal and Tim Horton on defense, there were no stars on the club. There had been five coaching changes since Day in 1950. The last change was to bring another great era to Toronto—"Punch" Imlach took over in 1959 as coach and general manager.

Imlach soon acquired Red Kelly, an All-Star defenseman with Detroit, and made him a center. He got Johnny Bower, whom the Rangers considered too old, as a goalie. And from the farm system he got Frank Mahovlich, Dave Keon, Carl Brewer, Bobby Baun, and Bob Pulford.

Imlach manipulated his talent with little concern as to how the players liked it. His object was to produce. He acquired older men from other teams—castoffs considered past their prime—and got another year or two of playing out of them. Although players such as Mahovlich and Brewer—both All-Stars—never really approved of his coaching techniques, Imlach produced powerhouses. In his first full season as coach, the 1960-1961 campaign, his club moved from fourth to second. A year later, it won the Stanley Cup, which it was to repeat two more consecutive times. Imlach

demanded constant work from his players, and their style, which infuriated the opposition and the opposing fans, was known as "clutch-and-grab." It worked, though. Imlach's reign ended in 1969, after four Cup champions. It came following a humiliating four-game defeat in the first round of Cup play against Boston. Stafford Smythe, who had taken over the club from his father, went in to see Imlach within minutes of the defeat, and announced to the press, "Gentlemen, the Punch Imlach era is over."

The Leafs hired a new general manager, Jim Gregory, and a new coach, John McLellan, to lead the team into what it hoped was a new era. It had some classy players in Keon and Norm Ullman, acquired from Detroit. It finished last in the 1969-1970 season, but bounced back to fourth in the 1970-1971 campaign, as a crop of young defensemen came up.

One of the more intriguing Leaf players was Mike Walton, nicknamed "Shakey." He was married to one of Smythe's nieces and was considered a promising player. But he was unhappy in Toronto and the Leafs refused to trade him. In a rare and dramatic move, Walton got a psychiatrist to certify that the player was suffering emotional stress by playing for the club. It prompted the league president, Clarence Campbell, to ask the Leafs to trade the young center. The club finally acceded, and a three-day deal, involving Philadelphia and Boston, evolved, with Walton winding up with the Bruins. In exchange, Bernie Parent, the Flyers' goalie, went to Toronto. Parent and Jacques Plante formed a top goaltending combination and the Leafs again finished fourth in the 1971-1972 campaign. Their future was clouded after the season, though, when they were hard hit by raiding parties from the WHA. Parent was the first name player to be plucked from the established league.

CHAPTER IV

The Great Expansion

From 1942 until 1967, the NHL remained constant with six clubs, even though baseball, football and basketball had all greatly expanded during those years. It took the threat of a rival league, which would use the burgeoning West Coast as its focal point, to move the NHL to action. In 1965, it announced it would expand by 1967. But it would do more than simply add one or two teams—it would double its size to 12 clubs and add a whole new division.

There was sound logic in this concept. If all the new clubs were in a separate division, they wouldn't have to worry about finishing far behind the established teams. Baseball had seen the error of expansion when it created the New York Mets and expected the club to compete as an equal. It took nearly a decade for the Mets to move out of last place. A new six-team hockey division also insured the West Coast of representation—and did away with the threat of a rival league.

Six franchises were awarded: to St. Louis, Philadelphia, Oakland, Los Angeles, Pittsburgh, and Bloomington, Minnesota, in the St. Paul-Minneapolis area. The new division was called the West Division, while the established clubs were called the East Division. Each new team was required to pay two million dollars for a franchise. The

cost, of course, covered the drafting of players from established teams. The draft, a remarkable accomplishment and the largest of its kind ever staged in the world of sports, was held in June, 1967, in Montreal. Each of the established clubs was permitted to "protect" two goaltenders and 12 players—these were the "untouchables." Then each new club chose a player from an established team. The routine was repeated until each expansion club had chosen 20 players, including two goalies, and each established club had lost 20 players, including the goalies.

The 1967-1968 season saw the expansion teams on the ice for the first time. What they lacked in talent they sometimes made up for in determination. Their styles usually were formless, and veteran fans, accustomed to seeing the 120 best North American hockey players on only six teams, now were watching 240 players of varying ability on 12 teams. But determination won out time after time and by the end of the season the West Division had surprised even itself by winning 40 games and tying 18 of the 144 played against the established East Division. Clarence Campbell, the league president, had indicated he would be satisfied if the new division won only 30 games.

Over the next few years, play deteriorated—instead of improving—in the new division. The league, however, made plans to expand even further, adding two more teams for the 1970-1971 season. Meanwhile, it wanted to polish up the West Division's fading image. The only way it could be done was to place at least one East Division team into the West. But which team? The choice wasn't that difficult. The Black Hawks finished last in the East during the 1968-1969 season. A move to the less powerful West would do wonders for the club and again make them competitive. So the league agreed that, starting in 1970, the Hawks would move. But before they did, the Hawks surprised everyone by leaping from last place to first in the East during the 1969-1970 season.

Thus, the Hawks entered the West Division, not as losers, but as champions. The two new clubs added during the 1970-1971 season were the Buffalo Sabres and the Vancouver Canucks. They were both placed in the East Division, creating two seven-team divisions. Only three years before, a new franchise had cost two million dollars, but the going price in 1970 was six million.

"It's not that a franchise now is worth three times what it was three years ago," said Campbell. "It's just that the teams that came in three years ago didn't pay enough. They got a bargain."

No one expected further expansion for at least a few years—until 1974. Even the league itself admitted it wasn't a wise idea to expand further. But the threat of the WHA changed all that. Late in 1971 the league suddenly decided to entertain thoughts about franchise additions for 1972. Finally, it awarded franchises to Long Island and Atlanta. Not by any coincidence, both areas had been courted by the World Association. It was obvious the established NHL wanted to beat the WHA there. The NHL knew that a New York

outlet was essential to any league's success, and if it could get in a second team in the New York area it would effectively hurt the upstart league's chances. So it gave New York a second team. This was the first time since 1942 that the league had two clubs in the same area. Atlanta was also important to the NHL, for it marked the first time a city in the Deep South had a big-league hockey team.

When the 1972-1973 season began, there were 16 teams with the two additions. Still further expansion was expected for 1974 by adding Kansas City and Washington, and by the end of the decade the NHL was talking of a 26-team league.

Atlanta Flames

"The ice age is coming to the South." That was the slogan the Atlanta team's advertising agency used to entice fans to think hockey. The South, apparently, was ready. Atlanta greeted the new team warmly.

The club was the brainchild of Tom Cousins, a highly successful businessman and real estate developer. He specialized in rebuilding urban areas, and one of his ideas is that an arena with major-league teams helps upgrade a city. His organization set about putting up an ultra-modern building called the "Omni," which means "all" in Latin. It was to be all-inclusive. Any major arena today must have a hockey team, though. Cousins got in touch with Bill Putnam, a banker specializing in sports franchises, who had been the first president of the Philadelphia Flyers and had also helped get the Los Angeles Lakers basketball team for Jack Kent Cooke, the West Coast impresario. With Putnam as president, and Cousins and other wealthy businessmen backing the club, Atlanta had

(Manny Rubio)

Dennis Kearns (6) of Canucks pins Bob Leiter of Flames against the boards.

little trouble getting a franchise from the National League.

Yet, there was hardly a hockey tradition in the city. Atlanta's rink measured 50 feet in length. The only other rink was 60 miles away, in Macon. So an advertising agency was hired to make people aware of this strange sport.

One of its schemes was to run a state-wide contest to choose a name for the club. More than 10,000 entries poured in and the name "Flames"—for the fact that Atlanta was nearly destroyed by fire in the Civil War—was the winner. The contest made thousands of people aware that a new team was coming to Atlanta.

Putnam named Cliff Fletcher, who had been with the St. Louis Blues as general manager. Putnam needed a coach to lead and inspire a newly formed club and his choice was a surprise—Bernie ("Boom-Boom") Geoffrion. The former Canadiens' star had been a coach with the Rangers for only four months before being forced to the sidelines with a bad ulcer condition. If the Boomer had stomach trouble with a contending team such as the Rangers, how would he react to the almost certain

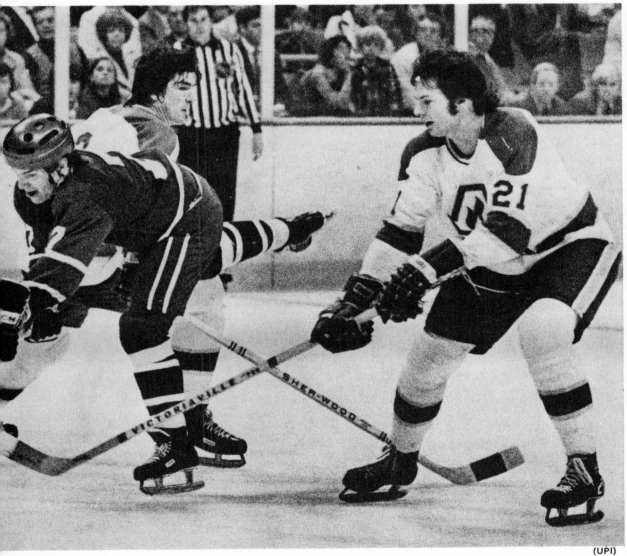

(UPI)

Atlanta's Pat Quinn (left) and Larry Romanchych (21) trip up Vancouver's Gregg Boddy.

losing record a first-year team would produce?

"He's not under pressure in Atlanta," explained Putnam after making his choice. "We don't expect a winner right away. We want someone to lead the team and give it self-respect." Geoffrion, who speaks English with a French-Canadian accent, took Atlanta by storm. At banquets he would tell the fans, in a Southern drawl, "Y'all come down to see us, ya hear?"

Although Putnam wanted scoring for his new club, he found that expansion players who were left unprotected in the draft would not be great scorers. Putnam had remembered his years with the Flyers, when Philadelphia was one of the lowest-scoring outfits in the league. "You've got to score goals to get some fans," said Putnam. But he couldn't find any goal-scorers, so he went for good goaltending and defensemen and wound up with Phil Myre from Montreal and Dan Bouchard from Boston as his goalies. On defense he selected Pat Quinn from Toronto, Randy Manery from Detroit, and made a deal to get Noel Price. In the amateur draft the Flames chose second and picked Jacques Richard, who they hoped would one day become their top goal-scorer.

By the time the season started, the Flames had sold more than 7,000 season seats. The South, especially Atlanta, appeared willing and able to accept hockey. The Flames helped by playing at .500 the first fourth of their season, a remarkable accomplishment.

Kerry Ketter (center) and Noel Picard of Atlanta close in as Seals' Stan Gilbertson (left) and Hilliard Graves (on ice) struggle for puck.

Buffalo Sabres

"I don't want a town named Buffalo playing in my building."

That was the attitude of one club owner when Buffalo made an unsuccessful bid to enter the league in 1967. But by the time their first season ended early in 1971, the Sabres had gained a good reputation, winding up fifth in the East Division. They beat out the other new entry, Vancouver, as well as the established Red Wings. Only eight clubs in the 14-team league had better records than the new Sabres.

For years, Buffalo had proved it could support a hockey club. The Memorial Auditorium had been the home of the Bisons, a successful American Hockey League squad. Canada was just across the border, and a substantial number of Canadian fans attended all the Buffalo games. Perhaps the road to the NHL for Buffalo began one day in 1965 on a golf course in Canada. Freddie Hunt, the Bisons' general manager, was playing golf with Seymour Knox, III, a member of Buffalo's first family with interests that included the Marine Midland Bank and Woolworth's. Hunt suggested that a major-league franchise would be an asset to their city.

Seymour discussed the prospect with his brother, Northrup—and their enthusiasm grew. The Knox brothers are among the world's top amateur athletes. Northrup had been the world court tennis champion, and is a top polo player—a former captain of the United States polo squad. Seymour had a worldwide reputation as a squash racquets competitor.

The brothers discovered, however, that it was easier to play than to field a team. Too many forces conspired against them, the most imposing of which was the city of Toronto. The Maple Leafs play only a hundred miles from Buffalo, and Toronto didn't want its television market affected by a competitive club. The Knoxes were disheartened as they were forced to watch the 1967 expansion from the sidelines. They invaded hockey soon afterward, though. The California Seals had fallen into financial trouble, and the Knoxes invested in the team, hoping to move it eventually to Buffalo. The league was willing to accept help, but said they couldn't move the club.

Patience paid off for Buffalo. Late in 1969, they were awarded one of the two new franchises for the 1970-1971 season. On January 16, 1970, the Sabres made their first major announcement: they had acquired a new general manager and coach. The man to fill both roles was, ironically, George ("Punch") Imlach, who had been fired from Toronto. The Sabres (a name chosen in a contest) were off to a good start.

Now Imlach had to get players. Although the Sabres had paid a one-million-dollar indemnification fee to the Bisons, the Bisons didn't have any players who figured in Imlach's plans. The coach would have to get his players through the draft.

The hockey world knew that the No. 1 amateur player in Canada was Gil Perreault. Anyone choosing first in the draft was sure to grab him. The first choice would go to one of the new clubs, either Buffalo or Vancouver.

A simple spin of a wheel of fortune would decide which club got the right to choose first. Imlach won. Without wasting a second, he named Perreault, and the Sabres were on their way. Then, a flip of a coin was to determine who would go first in choosing players from the established clubs. Imlach won again. He picked Tom Webster from Boston, and immediately traded Webster to Detroit for Roger Crozier, a good goalie. Thus, with two lucky breaks, Imlach acquired the best young player and the best goalie available.

Randy Wyrozuk of Buffalo hooks Larry Johnston of Leafs to keep him from puck.

(UPI)

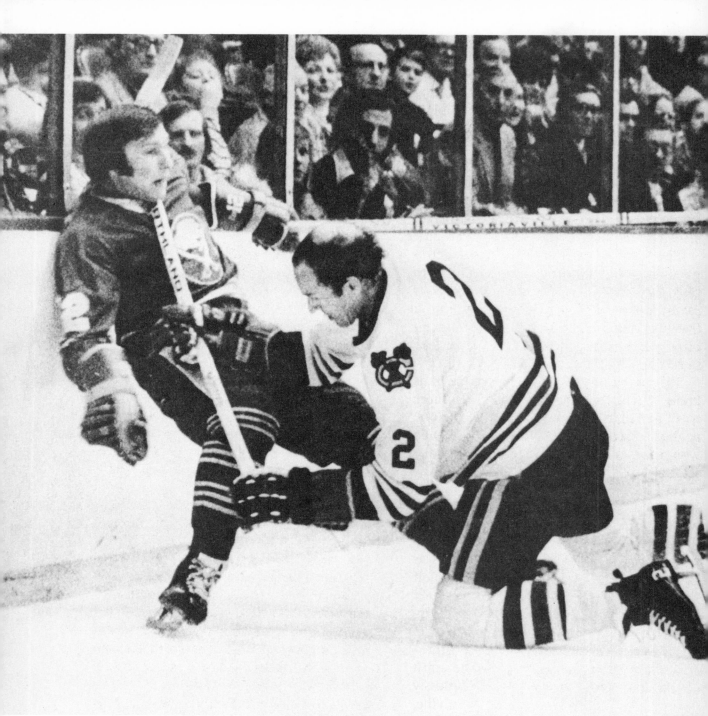

Buffalo's Larry Mickey is rapped across the neck by Black Hawk's Bill White. (UPI)

The remainder of the squad was made up of some interesting and colorful players: Eddie Shack, nicknamed "The Entertainer," who once walked into a training camp barefooted and wearing Bermuda shorts; Reg Fleming, a heavily penalized player, who admitted that if it weren't for his ability to hit he never would have remained in the league; Phil Goyette, a seasoned center, who was one of the game's smoothest performers; and Don Marshall, also an older player, who never got rattled.

The early games weren't particularly good ones. Marshall and Goyette refused to play, holding out for more money. Perreault looked as if he could develop into a true star, but Imlach had difficulty finding other players who deserved to be on the same line with the young center.

Still, it was a new team, and the fans knew they'd have to be patient. If there was one "must" game, it would be the one against Toronto—the first time Imlach would face his old team. It came when the season was six weeks old. Prior to the game's start at Maple Leaf Gardens, Imlach said to his players, "Look, you guys know what this game means to me."

Imlach sent the players out. Dramatically, he delayed his own entrance. He was missing from the bench as the first face-off was about to begin. Just as Referee John Ashley was about to drop the puck, Imlach appeared. The crowd spotted him in his white felt fedora, and gave him a standing ovation. Caught up in the spirit of the occasion, the Sabres relentlessly downed the Leafs, 7-2. Stafford Smythe, who had fired Imlach, didn't even wait for the game to end—he left the scene. In the closing seconds, the fans stood and shouted, "We want Punch!" When the game ended, Imlach tipped his hat to the crowd and walked jauntily down the exit ramp to the locker room. He remarked later, beaming, "My players said it for me."

That was the high point of an unusually successful first season. Perreault became the highest-scoring rookie in league history, with 38 goals and 72 points. Imlach continued to build after the season ended. He stunned the hockey Establishment with some fancy maneuvering at the intra-league drafts in the summer of 1971. Having discovered a loophole in the league rules, he was able to acquire five players while losing only one. Imlach also was going to institute the style of play that had made his Toronto teams so successful. "We're going to be the first expansion to win the Stanley Cup," he promised. Not many people laughed.

It didn't seem possible that Imlach would come up with another potential superstar in consecutive drafts, but that's exactly what happened. This time his amateur find was Richard Martin, who wasn't even the top selection and was passed over by other clubs. But Martin eclipsed even the great Perreault's rookie marks and scored 44 goals. He might have had 50, joining hockey's most select group, but a late-season injury hampered his chance. Imlach was forced to watch his team from the sidelines. A heart attack temporarily stopped him, and he picked his old friend, Joe Crozier, to direct the team.

By the time the 1972-1973 season rolled around, Imlach was back in his office as general manager, although he had turned over the coaching to Crozier. Perreault, Martin, and a fellow named René Robert, acquired in a trade late the previous season with Pittsburgh, came alive, and through the early weeks were the leading scoring line in the league. Buffalo, in fact, kept pace with the Montreal Canadiens the first month. They were one of the best-conditioned clubs in the league and had extraordinary confidence. Imlach's remarks suddenly didn't seem so far-fetched.

The Sabres went on to make the playoffs that season, and extended the Canadiens to six games before bowing.

California Golden Seals

The Seals have set records for crises that may never be broken. At various times, they have not known what their name was, where their paychecks were coming from, who was running the club, or who was playing.

There were several reasons why a franchise was desirable for the Oakland-San Francisco area. Geographically, it is one of the most important regions in North America—a huge population is clustered in a relatively small area. Certainly, there were enough fans to fill an arena. And there was television—any network that televised league games would be interested in the Bay Area because the people would be sure to watch the telecast. Of course, given a choice, the league would have chosen San Francisco. But the arena in San Francisco, the Cow Palace, didn't meet NHL standards. If a club were chosen to play in the arena, the NHL wanted it to perform in the Oakland-Alameda Coliseum. But that didn't pose much of a problem. After all, San Francisco was only an hour's drive away, and furthermore, there were a million people in the Oakland area alone.

As a means of getting a foot in the door, Barry van Gerbig, a society man-about-town from New York, convinced half a dozen friends to buy the San Francisco Seals of the Western Hockey League. When expansion came, van Gerbig, who had many friends in the NHL, knew he'd get the Bay Area franchise. He did, and the headaches started. The club couldn't be known as the San Francisco Seals, since it didn't play in San Francisco. The NHL

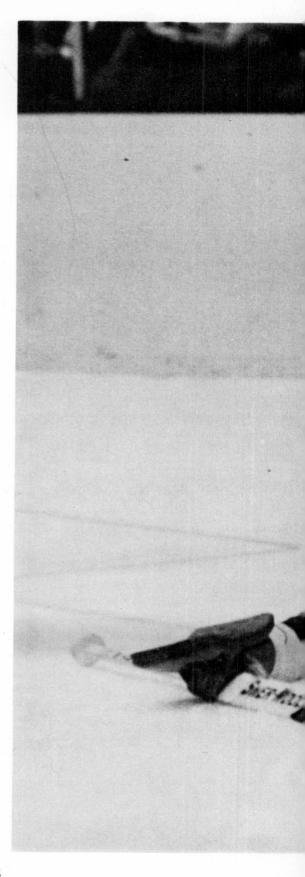

Marv Edwards of Seals sprawls full-length as puck sails over his stick.

(Arthur N. Anderson)

didn't want it known as the Oakland Seals, since Oakland didn't have a major-league image throughout the rest of the nation. So the club became known as the California Seals.

Oakland's residents felt slighted. If their city was good enough to host a hockey club that called itself big-league, why couldn't the team carry its name? If the fans were confused, consider the plight of the players. They didn't know who their boss was. Rudy Pilous, a long-time hockey man, had been hired as the general manager and coach, with Bert Olmstead, a former player known as Dirty Bertie, as his assistant. But a month before the critical draft meeting was to be staged, van Gerbig fired Pilous. Olmstead suddenly was thrust into the role of general manager. He had to pick 20 players and was ill-prepared to make knowledgeable judgments, so he did not do well in the draft. The Seals wound up with a rather poor collection of players.

If the fans had turned out for the games, the situation might not have been so bad. But they didn't. Sometimes it seemed as if there were more hot dog vendors than fans in attendance. Money problems piled up. The team's backers discovered they had to keep pouring money in just to meet expenses. New promotions to attract Oakland fans were tried, and before the team was two months old, the club's name was changed to the Oakland Seals. Management had given up any hope, for the time being, of attracting fans from San Francisco.

Things were just as bad on the ice as off. The team went through a 13-game losing streak, and had another interval when it didn't win for 11 games. While the rest of the new division was fairly evenly matched, the Seals were the only new team completely out of the running. Olmstead was dismissed as coach, and Gord Fasho-

way took over—the Seals' third coach in their first season.

The league loaned the team more than $250,000, and a Canadian brewery loaned it more than $600,000. The brewery hoped to be able to acquire the club and move it to Vancouver if the franchise were permitted to shift cities. The bickering and front-office problems were reflected in the way the players performed. The team won only 15 out of 74 games.

Several major changes were made, and in its second season the team performed much better. It was sold, first of all, to a group that also owned the Harlem Globetrotters, the clowns of basketball. Van Gerbig stepped aside and was given an advisory role. Olmstead was dismissed as general manager, and Fred Glover took over as coach. Bill Torrey, a long-time hockey and arena executive, became executive vice president and began a series of sweeping changes to turn the franchise around. Frank Selke, Jr., who had been the president, became the general manager. The Seals acquired Carol Vadnais, a youngster who could play left wing and defense, and he became the heart of the team. The Seals leaped to second place, winning 29 games. During the season, the Knox Brothers of Buffalo invested in the club. They hoped to move it to Buffalo. In the 1969-1970 season, the Seals again made the playoffs, finishing fourth. They had a good goalie in Garry Smith, a tall blond fellow who enjoyed stick-handling. Once, he brought the puck to mid-ice in an attempt to score a goal when the opposition's netminder was off the ice. Because of him, the league ruled that a goalie could not cross the middle of the ice.

Walt McKechnic of Seals takes header over Jim Schoenfeld of Sabres. (UPI)

(Arthur N. Anderson)

The Seals by this time were owned by Trans-National Communications, an entertainment conglomerate. But the economy turned sour, and TNC had trouble paying its bills. The league wanted to rid itself of TNC, but had to find someone willing to take over the club.

Two major parties were interested: Charles O. Finley, the single-minded owner of the Oakland Athletics baseball team, who had fired a manager for every year he owned the club, and Jerry Seltzer, whose father had founded the Roller Derby. Like van Gerbig, Finley had close ties with many important people in the league. Seltzer did not. Before an important talk with the league's board of governors, Seltzer cut his long hair "to make a better impression," but that didn't help. Finley was chosen.

One of Finley's first acts was to dismiss Selke and appoint Glover to the dual posts of coach and general manager. Then Finley changed the team's name to the California Golden Seals. But the team disappointed him. It posted the worst record in the entire league, gaining fewer points than the two new clubs during the 1970-1971 season. Many clubs were interested in Vadnais, and it was obvious the Seals would have to engineer a major trade to acquire players. They had traded away many top draft choices and no one was certain where help would be coming from.

96

Marv Edwards in acrobatic action.

Don Awrey of Bruins stretches to hold back Norm Ferguson of Seals from puck.

(UPI)

Soon, everyone in the front office left or was dismissed. But Garry Young, a young general manager who was able to go along with many of Finley's notions, stayed. Young brought in the youngest team in the NHL—virtually all the players were under 25 years of age. In the 1971-1972 season they helped the Seals become contenders. Among the keys was Gilles Meloche, a 21-year-old goalie, who was very emotional. Indeed, in one game in Madison Square Garden he was strafed with so many shots and goals that Young went to the bench and ordered Coach Vic Stasiuk to remove the goalie. Meloche went to the bench and began to cry. But he got over it and so did his club. The Seals were in playoff contention until the last weeks of the season, when youth and inexperience showed in the clutch games. Yet, they banked on the return of Tom Webster, a proven young goal-scorer who was sidelined with an injury; Bobby Sheehan, a 20-goal man; Norm Ferguson, who once held the rookie goal-scoring mark; and Wayne Carleton, a proven big-leaguer. Unfortunately for the Seals, all of these players jumped to the World Hockey Association in the summer of 1972. Vadnais had been traded to Boston near the end of the 1971-1972 season and now the club was without a star. The Seals were right back where they had started—on the bottom with a minimum of quality players.

97

Los Angeles Kings

The Kings—from their name to their uniform colors to their arena—were the creation of one of sport's most dominant personalities, Jack Kent Cooke.

Cooke had the Midas touch in virtually all of his ventures—so, he reasoned, why not ice hockey? A Canadian, he established a hard-driving reputation. He successfully ran the Toronto baseball team, managed television stations and publishing empires, and sold soap and encyclopedias. Indeed, he was one of the most successful salesmen Canada had ever seen. He moved to the United States, became a citizen, and contemplated retirement at 50. The more leisurely life didn't suit him, though, so he returned to sports, using southern California as his base. With William A. Shea, he started to form the Continental League in baseball, a move that forced the sport to expand and was responsible for the birth of the Mets. Cooke also was part-owner of the Washington Redskins football team, and owned the Los Angeles Lakers of basketball, as well.

Acquiring an ice hockey team was a bit more difficult. The Western League franchise already was owned by Dan Reeves, a West Coast sportsman who believed that he had the right to an NHL franchise. Because of Reeves's close ties with the Sports Arena, Cooke was told that even if he did get a franchise in the NHL, he wouldn't be able to play in the Sports Arena. Cooke responded in typical fashion: he said he'd build his own arena.

And that's just what he set about doing, as soon as he received the franchise. More important than a building, though, were players. One of his first moves was to buy the Springfield Indians of the American Hockey League from Eddie Shore. This gave Cooke an immediate edge over most of the other expansion teams. He had a ready reserve of professionals waiting in the minors. Cooke was so smug about his acquisition that he announced, before he had drafted even one player, "The Los Angeles Kings will finish first in the new division." Remarks such as these caused some of the more reserved owners to grumble, but it did bring attention to the Kings.

Some interesting maneuvering began when the draft finally took place. Cooke had hoped to claim Red Kelly from the Maple Leafs, retire him, and then appoint him coach of the new Kings. Cooke claimed he had reached agreement with the Leafs, who were to let Kelly go. But the Leafs wouldn't part with Kelly, and kept him on their protected list. They claimed that Cooke had reneged on a promise not to draft Terry Sawchuk, the goalie. Sawchuk was the first player drafted, and Cooke had him. The Leafs and the Kings finally made a deal, and Kelly became Los Angeles property.

When the draft was over, some of the Establishment owners snickered at the choices that Cooke and his general manager, Larry Regan, had made. Except for Terry Sawchuk, not one player had completed a full campaign that year in the big leagues. Cooke remained unperturbed, and again announced that his Kings would finish first.

When the season started, Cooke's predictions appeared to be accurate. The Kings were first, practically from the opening face-off. By December, they had moved into their new home, the gaudy Forum, and they were on their way to pulling one of the great surprises of the year. Kelly was the patient leader, an unexcitable type who never screamed or cursed. Like most of his players, though, he found it difficult to adjust to the climate of California, so different from that of his native Canada. One understandably could not readily get into the right frame of mind for ice hockey

(UPI)

Ed Van Impe of Flyers hits Kings' Real Lemieux with stick, but no penalty was called.

Ralph Backstrom of Los Angeles tumbling to ice after Canucks' Bobby Lalonde connects with his stick and draws hooking penalty.

(UPI)

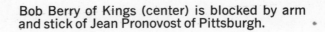
Bob Berry of Kings (center) is blocked by arm and stick of Jean Pronovost of Pittsburgh.

where sunshine and swimming pools abounded. For better or worse, the players made some sort of adjustment, but visiting teams never quite became accustomed to it, and the Kings posted the best home record of any expansion team. Their leading players were Bill ("Cowboy") Flett, who worked in rodeos in the off-season, and Bill White, a smooth defenseman.

In a virtual five-team battle for first place, the Kings held on most of the way, but on the final weekend the Philadelphia Flyers caught them. The Kings finished second, a point behind Philadelphia. They made the playoffs again in their second season, finishing fourth, as St. Louis established itself as tops in the new division. After the season, Kelly quit, following disagreements with Cooke. There was some club dissension as well. During the 1969-1970 season, the Kings went through two coaches, Hal Laycoe and Johnny Wilson, neither of whom could get any effort out of the Kings. White, one of the division's top defensemen, was traded. So was another good defenseman, Dale Rolfe, along with Gerry Desjardins, the goalie. The three had been particularly outspoken about their dislike of the Kings. The club finished last.

Larry Regan became coach for the 1970-1971 season, and good trades brought the team several good players. They included Juha Widing, a Finnish-born center, who became one of the division's leading scorers after coming from the Rangers. They also had Ralph Backstrom and Bob Pulford, two good and experienced players. The Kings dramatically improved their scoring. Late in the season, veteran Harry Howell joined them on defense and the club played at .500. The Kings again missed the playoffs, finishing fifth; their rebuilding, however, appeared to be in full swing.

Still, the Kings had defensive problems and they couldn't solve them in 1971-1972, when the squad slumped to last place. It yielded 305 goals, more than any other team in the 14-team league. Cooke did some more juggling and before the 1972-1973 season started he named Pulford as coach. Pulford immediately went to work instituting a style he knew had worked— the Toronto system. That meant the defensemen and forwards did more work, stopping the opposition at any cost. It was called "clutch-and-grab" hockey, and in the opening weeks of the season it worked. Bob Berry, Juha Widing, Ralph Backstrom, and Butch Goring played outstanding hockey as the scorers, and the defense, with Harry Howell, Gilles Marotte, and Paul Curtis, played solidly. In addition, Gary Edwards as the goalie performed well. The club got off to its best start despite spending most of the first month on the road. Yet, it set an expansion record by winning eight in a row and being undefeated in nine straight.

Mike Corrigan of Kings follows up his shot at Dan Bouchard, Atlanta goalie.

(UPI)

Minnesota North Stars

Of all the new clubs brought into the NHL, the North Stars play in the most hockey-minded part of the country. If there is a cradle of United States hockey, it is in Minnesota. There hadn't been many U.S.-born players by 1967 in the big leagues —only a dozen come easily to mind—but six of them were born in Minnesota.

So it was natural for a club in the state to receive a franchise. There was only one problem—where? The arena in St. Paul didn't measure up to NHL standards, and the arena between St. Paul and Minneapolis was inadequate, too. Behind the new franchise were: Walter Bush, a lawyer, who also coached the Minnesota Central League team; Gordon Ritz, a former Yale player, who was in the construction business; and Bob McNulty, a successful broadcasting personality. In order to obtain a franchise, these men had to show the league that they could put the team in a big-league arena. The Minnesota baseball and football teams already were playing in Bloomington, midway between Minneapolis and St. Paul. The three men convinced the Stadium Commission that an arena adjacent to the Stadium would make money. Once the Commission agreed to construct the building, the NHL franchise was approved.

To help fill the arena, an interesting plan was devised: they would play off the natural rivalries of St. Paul and Minneapolis. A group of businessmen from both cities ran a competition to see which city would sell more season tickets.

While the contest was in process, Wren Blair was hired as the new team's coach and general manager. Blair had been successful with the Bruins' organization, and more than any other man he was responsible for Boston's acquisition of Bobby Orr. Blair's first draft choice was goalie Cesare Maniago of the Rangers, who had fallen into disfavor in New York because he once had refused to continue playing after stopping a puck with his mouth. The Minnesotans tried for the best defensemen they could get, and weren't overly concerned with getting scorers. Ironically, defense turned out to be the team's problem. Rather than buying a farm club at first, Blair tried to get as many amateurs as he could. He also convinced Bill Masterton, an amateur who was working as an engineer, to turn professional.

It appeared to be an exciting season for the North Stars, who had several proven players in Elmer ("Moose") Vasko, Cesare Maniago, Dave Balon and Wayne Connelly. Nearly six thousand season tickets were sold. The early play of the North Stars justified their fans' confidence. They were in a close battle for first place for half the season. Their defense wasn't sharp, but Maniago was, and they had good goal-scorers. But on January 13, 1968, tragedy struck. In a game against Oakland, Masterton was hit by two players and landed hard on the ice. He was carried off to a hospital. Some of the players thought he was unconscious before his fall. Others recalled that a few games earlier he had complained of headaches. Whatever the cause, Masterton died within two days— the first fatality in the league's history.

The death caused far-reaching upheavals in the sport, whose equipment had changed little over the years. Almost immediately, many players started wearing helmets, and there was a drive to make helmets mandatory equipment. Stan Mikita's line at Chicago wore helmets, and Bobby Hull said that if he hadn't played without one for so long, he would wear one, too. Blair was perhaps the hardest shaken. It was he who had convinced Masterton to end a six-year retirement from the pro ranks.

No rules were changed regarding hel-

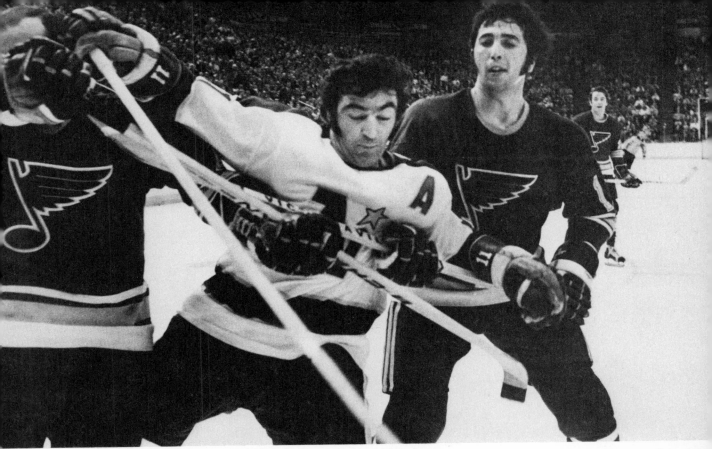

J. P. Parise, North Stars' left wing, checked by stick of Blues' defenseman.

Minnesota's Ted Harris swings at Atlanta's Bob Leiter as tempers flare.

mets, and after a few days the league continued on its way. But the Stars had been profoundly affected. The death had shaken every one of them, and many of them now wore helmets. The club lost six games in a row. It hung on to finish fourth, though—only four points out of first place—and made the playoffs.

In the first round of Cup play, the Stars faced the Los Angeles Kings, who got a huge edge by winning the first two games. But the Stars came back to take the series, four games to three, winning the last two games, including one in overtime. They faced the Blues for the right to meet Montreal for the Stanley Cup. The series went seven games, and there were four overtimes. In the final game, St. Louis won in the second overtime to eliminate the North Stars.

Blair remained as general manager, but he turned the coaching over to John Muckler as the North Stars began their second season with high hopes. They had a rookie, Danny Grant, coming up, they had received outstanding playoff scoring from Bill Goldsworthy, and there was a nucleus of solid scorers. But the North Stars went through a 14-game stretch in which they failed to win, and Wren Blair took over from John Muckler. The North Stars sank to sixth.

The poor team performance couldn't overshadow Grant's season. He tied the record for rookies with 34 goals, and was named rookie of the year. Blair was still behind the bench for the Stars' third season, and admitted that he was looking for a coach, "if I can find one." Blair said the problem of getting a coach was difficult to solve. "Today's players have to be treated differently from the way we were. They don't believe in the old-fashioned methods. You just can't order today's players to do something, you have to motivate them."

Still plagued by defensive difficulties,

Blair got his North Stars moving in their third season. After a while, he thought the time was appropriate for him to give up the coaching again. He named one of his players, Charlie Burns, as player-coach. But it wasn't long before Blair was back behind the bench again. Late in the season, he made a major deal when he acquired Lorne ("Gump") Worsley, the aging goalie from Montreal, to spell Cesare Maniago.

Blair finally found his coach for the 1970-1971 season: Jackie Gordon, one of the most successful executives in the minor leagues, who had also served for a time as assistant general manager of the Rangers. The North Stars produced the best goals-against average of their career, and made the playoffs, finishing one point behind the third-place Philadelphia Flyers. To lead the defense, they got the experienced Bob Baun late in the campaign.

Baun paid an immediate dividend. The Stars' first-round opponents in the playoffs were the St. Louis Blues, who had never been defeated in Cup play by a West Division team. The North Stars, led by Baun, had the honor of knocking them off.

In the second round, the Minnesotans' opponents were the formidable Canadiens. Baun, injured in the game against St. Louis, was unable to play. Still, the North Stars put on quite a show, extending the Canadiens to six games before losing. The Minnesotans appeared to have struck the right balance, finally, between defense and offense. They had a rookie "find" in Jude Drouin, who set a record for first-year men with 52 assists, and they had 30-goal scorers in Goldsworthy and Grant.

The North Stars proved they were on the rise in the 1971-1972 season when they become the second expansion team to finish a season at better than .500. They joined the St. Louis Blues in this respect when they wound up second to the Black

Jude Druoin of North Stars shoots and Pierre Bouchard of Canadiens defends.

Hawks in the West. Defense was the key as the club's 191 goals-against was the second best in all of the NHL. The goalies were Cesare Maniago, the ageless Gump Worsley, and the youthful Gilles Gilbert, as the Minnesotans employed a three-goalie system. The team was so far ahead of any other expansion team that it finished 19 points in front of third-place St. Louis.

There were no dramatic big-name scorers, but there was a solid list of players, including Bill Goldsworthy, Drouin, Lou Nanne, Jean-Paul Parise, and Dean Prentice. The experienced Ted Harris and Doug Mohns anchored the defense. It wasn't a young club, though, and even in victory Gordon was slowly rebuilding the team with more youthful players.

Gerry Desjardins, Islanders' goalie, watches the puck ricochet off his pad after successful block of shot taken by Ron Shock, Penguins' center.

New York Islanders

An instant team—that was the story of the Islanders, who came into the league in 1972. And when it was created it was the most expensive team in the history of hockey, costing more than $11 million.

Late in 1971 the World Hockey Association announced it would field a team in the virgin hockey territory of Long Island, once considered a suburb of New York City but now a self-contained affluent area with about a million people. The WHA realized, of course, that a New York franchise was essential to the success of a new league. What better place than in Long Island, in a brand-new big-league arena, the Nassau Coliseum? But the Coliseum authorities—most of them political appointees—wanted a major-league image for Long Island. They didn't like the idea of accepting only the second-best league. So they brought in William A. Shea, the man who brought the Mets' baseball team to New York, and for whom Shea Stadium is named. If anyone could bring big-league ice hockey to Long Island, the officials believed, it would be Shea. They weren't wrong.

Meanwhile, the NHL hadn't been giving too much thought to Long Island. For one thing, New York already was represented by the Rangers. But the National League obviously didn't want the WHA to succeed, and it knew that if it could bring off a team in New York, the rival league would have trouble getting off the ground.

That didn't deter a Long Island laywer named Neil Shayne. He was awarded the New York franchise of the WHA for $20,-000. Then he applied to the Coliseum for playing dates. The Coliseum stalled—it wanted the National League. A week after the WHA announced its New York franchise, the National League announced that *it* was going to add another team to New

Billy Smith of Islanders hits the ice in a futile attempt to stop goal by Atlanta's Lew Morrison. Randy Manery of Flames is at left. (UPI)

York—to play in the Coliseum! The move effectively undermined the WHA for Long Island. Strangely, the NHL franchise was awarded to the area of Long Island, not to a specific owner. Generally, a group of investors in a city is awarded the franchise, but the NHL was so intent on beating the WHA that it gave a franchise to a whole territory. Most people, however, knew that a sportsman named Roy Boe would really be the owner. It was simply a matter of his meeting the financial demands. The league wanted $6 million in franchise fees, and the Rangers wanted $4 million in indemnification for permitting Long Island to enter its 50-mile territorial radius. Boe and his backers eventually came up with the money and in December, 1971, his group was given the Long Island franchise of the National League to begin play in 1972. For the first time in 30 years—since

the New York Americans went out of business—the National League was going to have two teams in the same area.

Neil Shayne, annoyed at this situation, sued everyone connected with the league for millions of dollars. Eventually, he sold his territorial rights to the World Hockey Association to a group of New Jersey lawyers.

Roy Boe, meanwhile, had to field a team pretty quickly. He came to the game with almost no knowledge of the sport, although he was one of the keys of the American Basketball Association and owned the New York Nets. He considered a dozen chief executives and finally settled upon Bill Torrey, the former Seals' executive, under whose guidance the Seals had made the playoffs for the only two times in their history. Torrey was hired in February, 1972. He had no coach and no players. Many of those

110

Billy Smith, obscured by Greg Polis of Penguins who has rifled puck past him for Pittsburgh tally.

he would have liked to consider he wasn't permitted to approach until the 1971-1972 season was over. And other potential coaching choices turned him down.

So he went into the June draft meeting with no coach, an owner who couldn't help him make selections, and several aides he had known over the years. His first choice was a goalie, Gerry Desjardins, an expert netminder from the Chicago Black Hawks. Torrey's first choice of the amateurs was Billy Harris, considered Canada's top young player. Torrey selected defensively oriented players—players made available by other teams—in his 21 choices in the expansion draft.

"No one's going to give you a goal-scorer," he said, "so you have to try to find players with defensive skills and hope that you're smart enough to find the scorers among the amateurs."

But before the season began, the club was in trouble, as eight of his 21 choices, including his only experienced defensemen, were raided by the WHA. Billy Harris started off well, though. The right wing became the sport's highest-paid rookie, signing a three-year contract for $100,000 annually. Harris responded with five goals in his first seven games. But the Islanders had little scoring from others and their defense wasn't what they hoped it would be. Through the first fifth of their first season, the club won only two games.

"Now I've got to keep their spirits up," explained the coach, Phil Goyette, who had been selected just a few months before. "It's easy for a losing team to think it can't come back. I've got to convince them they can."

Only time would tell whether that philosophy worked.

111

Philadelphia Flyers

The Flyers' place in hockey history is secure—they were the first pennant-winning team in the West Division, and thus earned the Clarence S. Campbell Bowl. Before expansion had created the new division, the winner of the six-team league received the Prince of Wales Trophy. It was necessary, of course, to produce a suitable trophy for the winner of the new division.

The trophy was, at times, farthest from management's thoughts that first season. For openers, the Flyers had a more immediate problem. Their games were played in the new Spectrum, a building shaped like a sardine can. But a raging storm late in the season—while the Flyers were battling the Kings for first place—tore a huge hole in the roof. Seven home games had been scheduled for the critical month of March, the final month of the regular season. Five of those games had been assured of capacity crowds.

The day after the roof went, the Flyers were scheduled to play at home. They had no place to go. Luckily, Madison Square Garden was available for an afternoon game—the Rangers were playing that night. The Flyers faced the Oakland Seals before a remarkably large "neutral" crowd of 12,000 (all ticket-holders for that night's Ranger game were admitted free of charge). The Flyers player another "home" game at Toronto. Finally, they settled in Quebec City, the home of their farm team. In their last seven "home" games, they displayed a 3-2-2 record.

The accomplishment was extraordinary. At a time when they needed to be relaxed, they were just the opposite—living out of suitcases and playing without a home crowd behind them. But what they did couldn't be considered just luck. Careful planning had helped bring them to their divisional title, by one point.

The owners were Bill Putnam, a banker; Ed Snider, a sports promoter; and Joe Scott, a Philadelphia sportsman. Bud Poile, a discerning executive from the Western League, was named general manager, and Keith Allen, another West Coast man, was the coach. At the draft, the club picked up two young goalies from Boston: Bernie Parent and Doug Favell, who became the key to the Flyers' success. The team got other players, such as Ed Van Impe, a defenseman who had finished second to Bobby Orr as rookie of the year; Forbes Kennedy, a small but pugnacious center from Boston; Leon Rochefort from Montreal; and Brit Selby.

Another player picked up was Larry Zeidel. But he wasn't chosen in the draft. A defenseman passed up as too old by other clubs, Zeidel prepared a brochure listing his accomplishments and mailed them to all the clubs in the league. The Flyers were interested. Zeidel made the team. During the "home" game at Toronto against Boston, Zeidel suddenly took a swing at Eddie Shack. It was a tough brawl, with both players using their sticks freely. Later, Zeidel claimed that the Bruins had taunted him with anti-Semitic slurs. The league investigated, but no cause for action against Boston was found.

Remaining calm through most of the first-season storms were Doug Favell and Bernie Parent, who shared goaltending chores equally. During the first half of the season, they led the league in goals-against. Overall, they finished third, each turning in four shutouts. Although Parent posted a goals-against average of only 1.35—the lowest in the playoffs—the Flyers dropped their first-round series against the Blues.

By their second season, the Flyers attempted to gain more scoring punch. They brought together a trio, dubbed the "French Line," consisting of Jean Guy

Rick MacLeish, Philadelphia center, goes after rebound of his shot as Dave Dryden, Buffalo goaltender, keeps his eyes on the bouncing puck.

Gendron, Dick Sarrazin, and Andre Lacroix. But Favell was not quite as good as he had been the season before. The team's goals-against went up dramatically. The Flyers fell to third place. After the campaign, following a disagreement with management, Bud Poile left, and Keith Allen became the general manager. The new coach was Vic Stasiuk.

Stasiuk, a former player, believed that hockey players had to outfight the opposition in order to win. He demanded strong performances continually. The Flyers' scoring picked up, thanks to a rookie, Bobby Clarke, a daring player with good moves. The Flyers were virtually certain to make the playoffs. But they got only two points in their final eight games—and finished

fifth. They scored only 17 victories, but set a league record of 24 ties. Unfortunately, they didn't get any ties the last four games, and were shut out in their final two contests. One more point would have lifted them to the playoffs.

Clarke reached stardom during the 1970-1971 season with 27 goals, and Favell and Parent again were in good form. Late in the year, Favell was kept and Parent was traded to Toronto. The Flyers finished third. Intent on climbing even higher, the

Bill Clement's drive is deflected by
Roger Crozier of Sabres and Buffalo's
Paul Terbenche is checked into
the ice.

(UPI)

Flyers hired Fred Shero to coach in 1971. Shero had had a highly successful career as coach in the minors, and he promised to start with the fundamentals at Philadelphia.

Shero believed conformity was an asset, and one of his first edicts was: no long hair. "A team can't be made of individuals," he explained. But what the Flyers needed was goal-scorers, not haircuts; they scored fewer goals than anyone else in the league. Still, they appeared to have a playoff berth wrapped up. They went into the final game of the season in fourth place with a one-point lead over Pittsburgh. If the Flyers won, of course, it would be all over and they would clinch. However, if they tied and Pittsburgh won, then the Penguins would wind up with the identical won-lost-tied record, but would capture a playoff berth because they had taken the season's series from the Philadelphians. It appeared not to matter what Pittsburgh did. In the closing seconds the Flyers had a one-goal edge over the Sabres. But with four seconds remaining, Gerry Meehan scored and Buffalo tied the game. The Penguins, meanwhile, won their game, and the Flyers missed the playoffs.

An outstanding season for Bobby Clarke had been wasted. With 35 goals and 46 points, Clarke's 81 points were the second highest total ever achieved by a player on an expansion team. But only one other forward, Simon Nolet, scored over 20 goals, and that was the major cause of the Flyers' difficulties. Doug Favell's goaltending wasn't bad.

The Flyers appeared to rebound early in the 1972-1973 season with players acquired in trades—Bill Flett and Rick MacLeish. A rookie, Bill Barber, also was impressive. Clarke was still the scoring star, and finally, it seemed, the Flyers were going to have some goal-scorers.

Pittsburgh Penguins

Some big names were associated with the Penguins in their first season—Red Sullivan, Andy Bathgate, Earl Ingarfield. But the name of the club itself was the most interesting. It took a city-wide contest to come up with the winning entry, "Penguins." The name made Coach Sullivan wince. "A penguin?" he asked. "What kind of name is that for a hockey team?" The name probably was chosen because the club was going to play in the Civic Arena, a building known, because of its shape, as the "Big Igloo." Who might better play in an igloo than Penguins?

A syndicate of 20 people, led by State Senator Jack McGregor, brought the team to Pittsburgh. They selected a big name when they chose Jack Riley as general manager. Riley had been the president of the American Hockey League. Pittsburgh should have been an ideal place for a club; the season before expansion, the Pittsburgh Hornets of the American League had won the regular-season championship and the playoffs. Pittsburgh was a proven hockey town.

"That was part of the trouble," Riley admitted later. "My owners felt that the city was so accustomed to a winner, it wouldn't support a new club unless it could produce immediately." That is why Riley drafted one of the oldest teams ever assembled. The average age of the players was 31 years. "I had to get experienced players," he said. "I couldn't wait to develop the youngsters. I felt pressured to put out a winning team immediately."

As a result, players such as Bathgate, who had starred for the Rangers ten years earlier, were selected. Ingarfield was another ex-Ranger star. Ken Schinkel, a longtime minor-leaguer, was also brought in, as were Al MacNeil, an older defenseman, and Ab McDonald, who had been

Pittsburgh's Nick Harbaruk (11), Bryan Watson (5) and Darryl Edestrand (25) chase after the puck as Bobby Clarke of Flyers lands on the ice.

(UPI)

around for years. The goalie was a 31-year-old rookie, Les Binkley, who wore contact lenses.

Although the club started with many experienced players, it failed to get an early jump on the rest of the new division. They couldn't generate the enthusiasm that youngsters on the other new teams did, and their playing was mediocre. They were never even close to first the early part of the season—nor could they win consistently at home. That hurt them. Fans in most hockey cities expect even poor teams to win on their home ice.

Bathgate, however, was the surprise of the league. At age 35, he quickly became the division's leading scorer. McDonald also had a good season. And Binkley produced in the nets. The team finally started to move late in the season. But it wasn't soon enough; the Penguins finished fifth, out of the playoffs. Binkley wound up with

Duane Rupp (2) and Darryl Edestrand (25) of Pittsburgh get sticks on puck as they hem in Ralph Backstrom of Kings and Pittsburgh's Jim Rutherford stays alert.

(UPI)

six shutouts, second-highest in the entire league, and Bathgate led the division with 59 points. McDonald scored 22 goals. The Penguins won their last four games of the season, and it looked as if they might be on their way.

The Penguins' sagging attendance had scared off the owners, however. After the season, the majority interest was sold to a Detroit banker, Donald H. Parsons, who promised to keep the club in Pittsburgh "until the city proves it can't support a hockey club." During the off-season the Penguins did little to attract the fans—Bathgate was dropped and McDonald was traded, depriving the club of its only 20-goal scorers.

The moves were made so the club could institute a youth program. The fans were asked to be patient. They weren't. Attendance fell by 20 per cent and the Penguins again finished fifth, yielding a huge number of goals and not generating much scoring power.

At the start of the club's third season, Sullivan was dismissed. Red Kelly replaced him, following two successful seasons at Los Angeles. Kelly turned the goaltending over to Al Smith, a rookie, and used Binkley as a back-up. The club had a rookie "find" in Michel Briere, a center, and got a surprisingly good season from an old-timer, Dean Prentice. Under Kelly, the club leaped to second place. It had made the playoffs, having been the only expansion team out of the playoffs for either of its first two seasons.

The Penguins sailed through their first round of Cup play, topping the Seals in four straight games as Briere scored in overtime in the final game. Then they extended the St. Louis Blues to a six-game semi-final series, although the Blues had run away from the division during the regular season. Binkley returned to form during the playoffs and in seven games

posted an excellent goals-against average of 2.10. Briere had a fine playoff, scoring five goals in ten games. For the first time, the club and its fans were looking forward to the next season.

But a few weeks after the playoffs, Briere was critically injured in an automobile accident. He was the heart of the team, and Kelly found himself in a predicament. Kelly had also replaced Riley as the general manager, but was unable to find someone to take Briere's place. Bathgate rejoined the team, and had a good season playing part time. There was no leader, though, and the club slumped to sixth in the 1970-1971 season.

The club also had management problems. Parsons was unable to run the team, and the league took it over. Riley moved up the ladder to the club's presidency. When the 1970-1971 season ended, the Penguins learned that Briere had died.

Kelly kept up his club's spirits in the 1971-1972 campaign. Indeed, he established a sort of tradition of making the playoffs by winning the clutch games. The Penguins' victory on the final game of the season got them into the playoffs ahead of Philadelphia, marking the second time in his three seasons that the Penguins made the Stanley Cup competition. Kelly had some solid scorers—the club got more goals than the other seven expansion teams. Syl Apps, a smooth young center, was the playmaker, and there were 30-goal men in Greg Polis and Jean Pronovost. Ken Schinkel, an old-timer and a solid performer, also helped out with the scoring. Jim Rutherford was the goalie more often than not, and he posted a record of better than .500, even though the Penguins as a whole were 12 games below the break-even point.

The old Penguins had gradually reshaped their image, and were mixing the best of youth and age.

St. Louis Blues

What expansion needed was a winner —a club to make the new teams respectable. The Blues filled the bill. In the first four years of expansion, they were the only team to post a winning record. No other club ever posted a .500 record for one season.

The chief architect of this remarkable accomplishment was Scotty Bowman, a former player in the Montreal farm system whose playing career was cut short by a concussion. Before Bowman joined the Blues, the club had an interesting beginning. No one from St. Louis had made a bid for a franchise when the league announced it was going to expand.

But Chicago wanted a St. Louis team in the league. The Black Hawks owned the St. Louis Arena, an old building that was losing money. If a team were placed in St. Louis, the club would have to play in the Arena, and the building could be sold. So Chicago persuaded the league to give a franchise to St. Louis, though no one there had asked for one. One of St. Louis's leading citizens, Sidney Salomon, Jr., hadn't even considered buying a hockey team. But his son, Sidney Salomon, III, an avid hockey fan, had a talk with his father. The father listened to the son, and agreed to buy a team. When the St. Louis contingent approached the league's expansion meeting, it already had a name. The club would be called the St. Louis Blues. It got the franchise, and the Chicago Black Hawks got rid of an old building.

The Salomons selected Lynn Patrick as the team's general manager and coach, and Bowman was made his assistant. Patrick had one of the most extensive backgrounds in the game. An All-Star player with the Rangers, he eventually became New York's coach. After that, he was coach and general manager of the Bruins.

Patrick and Bowman looked for a defensively oriented team in the draft. Their goaltender was Glenn Hall, one of the best. Their scorers were not formidable, and their defense included Al Arbour, who wore glasses but wasn't afraid to go to his knees to stop an oncoming puck. Hall referred to Arbour as "my second goalie," and also remarked, "I know that I wouldn't want to stop those shots if I were wearing glasses."

The Blues didn't get many people excited after the first month of play. Fans were lukewarm, matching the club's performances. The team lost seven games in a row. In late November, Patrick turned the coaching over to Bowman. A week later, Patrick traded his leading scorer, the veteran Ron Stewart, for Red Berenson, who had amassed only two goals in 19 games. Bowman, however, remembered Berenson's potential when both had been at Montreal. Berenson hadn't scored in 30 games the previous season with the Rangers, and many observers thought the New Yorkers got the better of the deal. How wrong they were! As soon as he put on a St. Louis uniform and got a chance, Berenson became the club's spearhead. He killed penalties, he was on the power play—and he scored. The Blues also brought up two minor leaguers, Tim Ecclestone and Frank St. Marseille. Then the club lured Red Hay out of retirement. Bowman, who knew many of the old Montreal stars, also got Doug Harvey and Dickie Moore, former Canadien All Stars.

Bob Plager (5) and Barclay Plager (8) of Blues go into Philadelphia stands to battle with fans who pelted St. Louis Coach Al Arbour with trash.

(UPI)

Bob Johnson makes save for Blues as Boston's Mike Walton tries to crash through. **(UPI)**

Suddenly, the Blues had a perfect blend of age and youth, and they began to move. Berenson was in the forefront as St. Louis picked its way past more and more teams. Midway through the season, the most dramatic event of their short career occurred, and perhaps marked a turning point. They were playing at home before their largest crowd, against the Rangers. The New Yorkers took a 3-0 lead. But the Blues came back, tying the game and then winning it. From then on, they packed the house with fans. Despite their poor start, they finished third, only 3 points behind the Flyers, and had fewer losses than any other West Division club. Berenson, playing only 55 games, had 22 goals and a total of 51 points. He became acknowledged as the first superstar the West produced.

The Blues won another honor in the playoffs. They were the first West Division team to make it to the finals to battle for the Stanley Cup. They got past Philadelphia and Minnesota in a seven-game series and then faced the powerful Montreal Canadiens. The Blues gave a good account of themselves, forcing the Frenchmen into overtime twice. The four games, though swept by the Canadiens, each were decided by only one goal.

The Blues began their second season with a three-brothers act on defense—Barclay, Bill and Bob Plager. The three had reputations for fighting—among themselves, and with their father, the opposition, and friends back home. The club also picked up someone to share the goaltending with Hall: Jacques Plante. The former Canadiens' star had been retired for a few years, but he had remained fit, and welcomed the opportunity to return. In Plante and Hall, the Blues suddenly had two of history's finest netminders on the same club. Had old age caught up with them? Bowman, who had been made general manager, didn't think so.

He began alternating them when the season began. Whichever goalie wasn't playing was told by Bowman to relax in the stands, instead of sitting on the bench. On the ice, meanwhile, the Blues ran away from the rest of the division. Bowman could afford to play a few little jokes. Once, he put the three Plagers together as a forward line, just for laughs. The line was broken up after a few seconds when one of them drew a penalty.

Berenson achieved stardom, and St. Louis began packing the Arena for every game. But Berenson didn't receive true national recognition until November 7, 1968, at Philadelphia. That night he scored six goals. He was only the second man in the sport's modern era to do so, and included in his outburst was a record for one period of four goals. He became known as the Red Baron, and he lived up to the name of the German flying ace as he netted 35 goals and 82 points for that season. The Blues finished first by 19 points over Oakland.

In the playoffs the Blues again swept their series against their divisional opponents. Again they faced the Canadiens for the Cup—and again the Canadiens defeated them in four straight games. But the Blues had achieved many honors during the season. Their goalies, Glenn Hall and Jacques Plante, captured the Vezina Trophy for permitting the fewest goals, and Hall was named to the first-team All Stars.

If there was a weakness in the club, it was in scoring. Excellent defense and goaltending had kept the Blues on top. Bowman thought that if he could add some firepower, it would take the pressure off the defense and perhaps also enable the Blues to win the Cup.

Bowman made another deal with the Rangers, and received Phil Goyette, who was 36 years old. In spite of aches and pains, Goyette produced. In fact, in the early weeks of the 1969-1970 season, Goyette led the league. He was the first West player ever to appear on top of the scoring parade. As the season progressed, Bowman kept Goyette's appearances down, saving him for the playoffs. Luckily, Bowman had such an imposing lead in the division that he could afford to keep his leading scorer on the bench. Goyette accumulated 78 points, and also won the Lady Byng Trophy. Having been given up earlier as "too old," Goyette turned in the finest season of his career. The Blues wound up on top with a 24-point edge over the Penguins, one of the largest margins in league history. But in the playoffs, Goyette was far from his peak. The Blues again won the first two rounds, but bowed in four straight games in the finals—this time to the powerful Boston Bruins.

There was tension in the Blues' camp when the 1970-1971 season started. Chicago now was in the division, and it was obvious the Blues couldn't catch the Hawks, who had led the East Division the season before. Plante was traded to Toronto in a complicated deal involving New York, and Goyette was drafted by the new Buffalo team. Bowman turned the coaching over to Al Arbour. The other teams were ready to begin closing in on St. Louis.

As expected, the Hawks went out front early. The Blues were a solid second, but wanted to insure that position for a few years. Late in the campaign the Blues traded their hero, Red Berenson, to Detroit for Garry Unger.

It was the first time the public realized that there wasn't perfect harmony in the club. Another sign that the Blues weren't what they used to be appeared in the 1971 playoffs. They were defeated in the first round by Minnesota, marking the first time St. Lous failed to get into the finals. Bowman resigned and was replaced by Sid Abel, the long-time Detroit figure. When he left,

Bowman said, "Once the owners start to believe they know more hockey than the general manager, it's only a question of time before there's a split. I wasn't going to stay anyplace where I couldn't make the decisions." Patrick again became general manager.

Early in the 1971-1972 campaign it was apparent the Blues' dynasty was going to be short-lived. For the first time they were overshadowed by another expansion team, the Minnesota North Stars. Without much scoring, with Hall retired and Plante in Toronto, the Blues didn't have the one top player to lift them up when they needed it. The team rutted around the middle of the West Division. Then Abel was dismissed and Arbour took over. Some key trades were made and Jack Egers and Mike Murphy joined the Blues from the Rangers. Egers had one of the hardest shots in hockey, but had not been given much of a chance with the Rangers. In 63 games with the Blues, though, he got 21 goals, while Murphy got 20. Unger led the team with 36. The Blues started winning late in the season and lifted themselves to third.

But after a few weeks of the 1972-1973 season, the Blues again were foundering. This time Arbour was dismissed and Jean-Guy Talbot took over the coaching duties. The Blues no longer were in a class by themselves. They were going to have to struggle, like everyone else.

St. Louis goalie Ernie Wakely in a figure-8 dive for puck as Pit Martin of Black Hawks slams into him.

(Wide World)

Vancouver Canucks

Patience was rewarded for the citizens of Vancouver, who make up the smallest population center of any NHL city. They were dismayed to be denied a franchise during the great expansion of 1967, when the six new clubs added were in the United States. Canadians in general thought that their country should have had at least one new club in their favorite sport's major league.

For a time, Vancouver had hoped that the floundering Seals would be moved to Canada. But the league didn't want to be known as a "carpetbagger," or someone who moved whenever there was a chance to make more money in a new city.

In 1967, there were groups willing to invest two million dollars in a new franchise. By the time 1970 rolled around, though, new franchises were costing six million, and the buyers in Vancouver were not so anxious for this type of expense. The Western Hockey League already had a team in Vancouver, known as the Canucks. They were bought by an investment company that handled doctors' funds. The club's general manager was Joe Crozier, a friend of Punch Imlach's.

The owners of the Canucks were prepared to put up the money to get an NHL franchise. Imlach was ready to be the general manager and coach of the new entry. But Crozier got into a disagreement with the owners before the 1969-1970 season ended. He was fired, and Imlach stepped out of the picture. So when the owners were awarded an NHL franchise for the 1970-1971 season, they had to go looking for a general manager.

Bud Poile was a sensible choice. Poile, the first general manager of the Flyers, had been successful in the Western League as a coach and general manager. He took over the Western League Canucks in February,

Don Lever of Canucks checks Bob Plager of Blues from getting to the puck.   (Bill Cunningham)

1970. Hal Laycoe was chosen to finish out the season as their coach. The Canucks won their playoffs.

Now the new expansion team was ready to begin. Although they also were named the Canucks, they didn't have any championships. They had to start from the beginning, at the draft. Poile went into the draft good-naturedly. "A guy's got to be crazy to start an expansion team twice," he said. But with the same skill that had enabled him to mold the Flyers into a first-place club their first season, Poile set out to get a winner at Vancouver. He knew, of course, that the going would be rough. When he had headed the Flyers, that team was placed in a division with other new teams. The new Canucks, however, were to be placed in the established East Division, along with one other new team, the Sabres.

Poile kept in mind the mistakes other expansion clubs had made. He wanted to be able to select a team and put it on the ice without constant changes. "I needed a nucleus," he said, "a solid core that knew it would be playing game in and game out."

Vancouver's Dale Tallon uses stick to intercept Ron Stackhouse of Red Wings.   (Bill Cunningham)

First came the draft of junior players. Poile, who lost out in the first choice to Imlach of Buffalo, selected Dale Tallon as the second pick in the draft. Tallon could play defense and offense, and Poile compared him to Bobby Orr. Poile also needed a team leader, and he selected Orland Kurtenbach of the Rangers in the expansion draft.

Kurtenbach's selection was viewed with some surprise. He had managed to get only four goals in 53 games with the Rangers, and had been bothered with a bad back. But Poile had always felt a special fond-ness for Kurtenbach, since the days when Kurt played for Poile in San Francisco. The Canucks also acquired solid players in Pat Quinn, Wayne Maki, Andre Boudrias and Rosaire Paiement.

Vancouver was elated at the prospect of having an NHL team of its own. More than twelve thousand season tickets were sold before the season even began. The fans were rewarded. The Canucks started out strongly, and for a month they played at .500. The team was cohesive, as neither Poile nor Laycoe made any dramatic personnel changes. Kurtenbach was one of

Vancouver's Dunc Wilson is chagrined as drive by Penguins' Nick Harbaruk gets by him.

(UPI)

Vancouver's Gerry O'Flaherty, after getting off shot, is knocked off his feet by hard check from Bruins' Bobby Orr. Boston goalie is John Adams.

(Bill Cunningham)

the league's surprises. Never a particularly strong scorer, he was suddenly among the league leaders.

But in December, Kurtenbach was injured—and he remained out for a third of the season. The Canucks, before his injury, had given a lot of goals, but were often able to overcome the defensive lapses by their own scoring power. Without Kurtenbach, the team went into a tailspin. It picked up a bit by the end of the season. Six players scored 20 or more goals, and Paiement had 34. The team finished sixth, ahead of Detroit, and outscored seven other teams.

The club suffered the so-called sophomore jinx in its second year. Poile had been intent on keeping the opposition scoring down and selected a defenseman, Jocelyn Guevremont, as his top choice in the 1971 amateur draft. But the club's defense was young and inexperienced. He had to hope the scorers would come through. They didn't. "They must have been reading their press clippings," said Laycoe. "They're not putting out the way they were their first season. Maybe they thought they had already proved themselves."

The second season was a disaster. Only one team in the League scored fewer goals than the Canucks, and only one club yielded more goals. The Canucks wound up with lowest point total. Only three players on the team reached the 20-goal plateau.

"When you've got an expansion team and it doesn't win, the coach will be fired," said Laycoe. Sure enough, his prediction came true. He was dismissed after the season and replaced by Vic Stasiuk. The new coach knew he had the fans and the potential with some of his players. It was now a question of having patience until the club could start winning.

CHAPTER V

World Hockey Association

The rising interest in hockey and the rising cost of hockey franchises led eventually to the creation of the World Hockey Association. The prime movers were Gary Davidson and Dennis Murphy, both of whom had helped found the American Basketball Association, a rival to the established National Basketball Association. They knew something about the start-up problems of a new league.

For their troubles, they split $250,000, which was a sort of finder's fee. Ten clubs contributed $25,000 apiece to become members. Eventually, there were 12 clubs, following franchise shifts and franchise dropouts, before the league got on the ice in October, 1972. The new clubs found their costs considerably less than if they had attempted to join the National League. After the initial $25,000 contribution, each team put up $100,000 to help operate the league. Another $100,000 was assessed to guarantee salaries, and then another $50,-000 was put up, all of which came to under $300,000 a club, compared to the $6 million an NHL franchise would cost. In addition, the Canadian cities in the new league finally had a chance to go major-league. They would never have been considered big enough to receive a National League franchise.

The WHA teams, however, didn't get any players for their money. An NHL expansion team at least picked 21 players. So the WHA set out to get players by the only means possible—raiding them from the Establishment. Thus began the biggest money war in the history of sports.

It started with Bernie Parent, the goalie for the Toronto Maple Leafs. Parent hadn't signed a valid NHL contract. In essence, he was a free agent. The Miami Screaming Eagles of the new league got him for a $500,000, five-year deal. When the club folded, his contract was assigned to the Philadelphia Blazers. With all this money offered, the league gained a certain amount of respectability in the public's mind. Still, the NHL laughed at the upstarts and the public wasn't convinced it was for real.

Then came the Bobby Hull deal. At first it seemed a joke to most people. The WHA had held a draft and the Winnipeg Jets selected Bobby Hull as their first choice. No one paid any attention to the selection, though. How could a new league possibly match the established league's salary? Yet, Ben Hatskin, the owner of the Jets, was serious. He began hard negotiations with Hull, and with Hull's accountants and lawyers. The Jets made an offer, and Hull then went back to the Hawks to see whether the Chicagoans could do as well. This is the way it went, back and forth, and the public was both amused and curious. Then, one day, the sports world was shocked. In a deal of such gigantic proportions that it had to be signed in two countries, Hull jumped to the upstart league. He got the unbelievable sum of $1 million as a cash bonus and signed a 10-year deal as player-coach for an additional $2.75 million. With the signing, Hull became the first athlete in the world ever to receive such a bonus, and one of the highest-salaried players in the world of sports—if not the highest.

Outrageous salaries and outrageous salary demands now became the order of the day. The National League, meanwhile, was convinced that its reserve clause—the controversial few words that bind a player to a team for as long as the club wants his services—was legal. Still, the established league was worried. The owners agreed that they would stand firm and not accede to players' requests for gigantic salary leaps. That didn't deter the players. A minor-leaguer from the Bruins' chain, Ron Plumb, jumped to the Philadelphia Blazers for a contract worth more than $60,000 a year. He had been earning $10,000 in the minor leagues. The Rangers' top goal-scorer, Vic Hadfield, was offered $1 million to play four years, and Brad Park, the club's top defenseman, received a similar offer from the WHA.

The heaviest negotiating transpired between the Bruins' Derek Sanderson and the Blazers. Finally, Sanderson topped even Hull's salary. In fact, he became the highest paid player ever, even though he had never led the league in any scoring department except shorthanded goals. But he had excitement and was a drawing card, and that's what the league wanted. He agreed to play for five years for $2.65 million— more than half a million dollars a year. "They made me an offer I couldn't refuse," said Sanderson.

Many of the NHL teams refused to get into the bidding war. But not the Rangers. They believed that with all the jumping going on they could win themselves a Stanley Cup by meeting the demands of their stars, since the other top contenders had lost several of their stars. So the Rangers signed Hadfield to a five-year deal worth about a million dollars, and gave the same to Park. Rod Gilbert and Jean Ratelle also signed for close to that figure, while Walt Tkaczuk signed for more than $100,000. Just two years before, Tkaczuk and Park each had earned about $12,000. Many of the other clubs in the NHL were annoyed with the Rangers, who they claimed had violated the secret agreement not to raise salaries to spectacular amounts.

When all the raiding was over, about 60 players had jumped from the NHL to the WHA. In addition, dozens of minor leaguers also had made the big leap.

Although the reserve clause was in question, there was no argument that the players from the NHL were under contract to their old teams until September 30. The standard contract ran from October 1 of one year to September 30 of the next. Yet, the WHA season was to begin on October 11. That meant there would be no training camp for the established players, since they weren't permitted to skate with their new clubs until October 1. They had only a little more than a week to prepare for the season. Hull, however, wasn't permitted to start— the Black Hawks obtained a restraining order against him, based on the reserve clause. After a few games, a Federal judge in Philadelphia lifted the order. Then it went back and forth between courts to decide whether he could play.

But the WHA believed it was here to stay. It tried to create an exciting, high-scoring image. There was to be an orange puck, instead of the traditional black. There would be overtime games, in the event of a tie. There would be no icing permitted from inside a shorthanded team's defensive zone. The orange puck didn't work out. It came apart. A blue puck was substituted, and when it didn't freeze, that problem was worked out, too.

The following are the teams that began the new league's first season.

(Murray MacGowan)

Alberta Oilers

The self-styled "Mr. Hockey of Western Canada," Bill Hunter, was the guiding force behind the Oilers. Alberta was one of those Canadian cities without a chance to land an NHL franchise. Its arena, the Edmonton Gardens, held only slightly more than five thousand people, and it didn't have a large population base. Yet, Hunter believed Alberta could support big-league hockey at big-league prices. Hunter, the executive vice president and general manager, selected Ray Kinasewich as coach. The squad signed such NHL players as Jim Harrison, Allan Hamilton, and Val Fonteyne. Hunter, who had run the Edmonton Oil Kings junior club, one of the top amateur outfits in Canada, also got many former juniors to play for him. It was a strong club, as the WHA went, and was among the leaders early in its first season.

Alberta's Ken Brown (above) is backed into the goal by his defenseman (on ice) after Tom Martin of Nationals scores and Roger Cote (2) of Oilers arrives too late. Brown and Allan Hamilton (3) (below) are on their guard as Wayne Carleton of Ottawa waits to take pass and shoot for a goal.

(Murray MacGowan)

Chicago Cougars

Ed Short, former general manager of the White Sox, became the hockey team's general manager. The club talked of building a large new rink in the Chicago suburbs, but began by playing in the International Amphitheater, an arena seating 9,000. The coach was a longtime NHL player, Marcel Pronovost. One of their first selections was Reggie Fleming, a crowd-pleasing bruiser who had played for the Black Hawks. They also got Rosaire Paiement, who had a 30-goal seaon as a Vancouver Canuck, as well as Larry Cahan and Jim McLeod.

Chicago's Bobby Sicinski (17) has scored against Jack McCartan of Saints. Cougars' Rosaire Paiement is on ice and Jan Popiel (19) of Chicago backs up play.

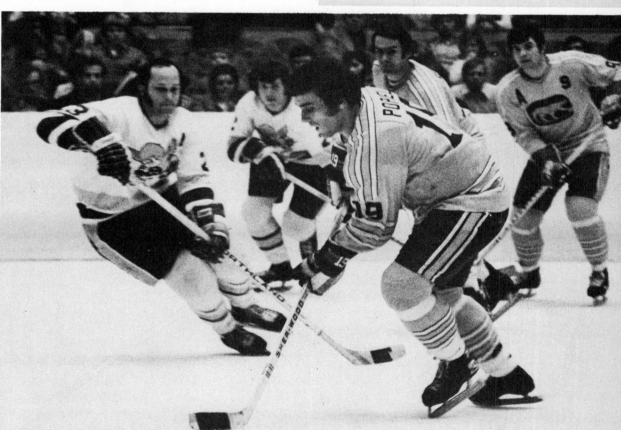

Jan Popiel of Chicago skates toward puck as Saints' Mike McMahan rushes over.

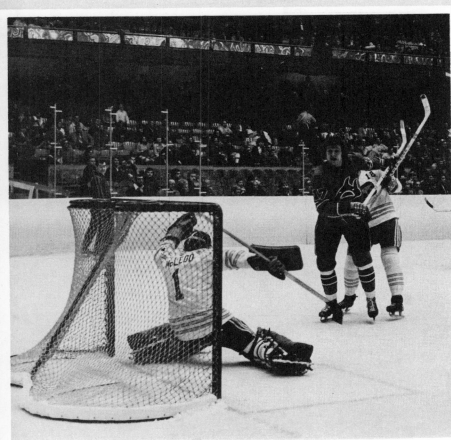

Jimmy McLeod of Chicago makes butterfly save to the dismay of Bill Young of Sharks.

Cleveland Crusaders

When he was turned down for an NHL franchise, Nick Mileti, a lawyer-sportsman, brought Cleveland into the WHL. He entered into intense negotiations with some of the Ranger stars, but finally landed a prize in Gerry Cheevers, the goalie for the Boston Bruins. Cheevers signed a six-year, $1-million deal, and became the most famous goaltender to jump leagues. The Crusaders also obtained Paul Shmyr and Gerry Pinder from the Seals.

Then Fred Glover, a former Seals' coach and general manager, became the team's personnel director. Ironically, a few weeks after he was hired he went back to the Seals as executive vice president and, eventually, coach. Thus, he was missing two of his key players who had jumped to a team he had worked for.

The Crusaders played at the Cleveland Arena, a 10,000-seat auditorium, but Mileti was busy making plans for a 17,000-seat building that would house not only his Crusaders but his Cavaliers of the American Basketball Association. In addition, Mileti also was president of the Cleveland Indians baseball team.

Cleveland's Ron Buchanan looks back after Quebec's Serge Aubrey blocks his shot and Jacque Blain of Nordiques heads for the puck.

(UPI)

Paul Shmyr's bid for Cleveland score just misses as puck hits outside of net. Guarding Quebec goal is Serge Aubrey, helped by J. C. Tremblay.

(UPI)

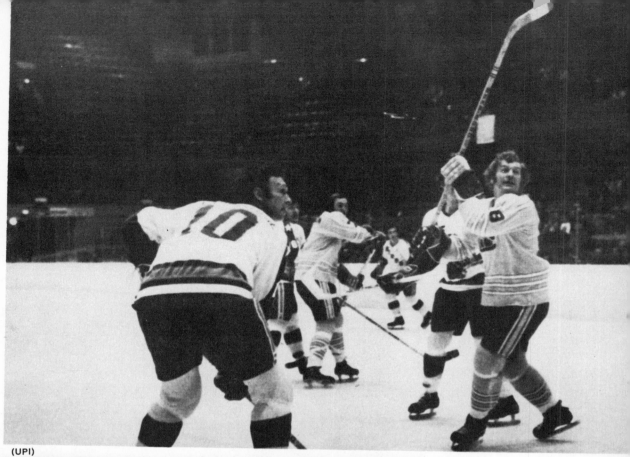

In his first WHA game, Bobby Hull slaps puck through legs of Gordon Kannegiesser, Houston defenseman, and registers his first goal for Winnipeg in third-period action.

Houston Aeros

The Sam Houston Coliseum, holding 9,000, was the site where Texas was introduced to major-league hockey. There had been a Central League team there for four years, so the fans knew something about this foreign game. Jim Smith was the general manager and Bill Dineen was the coach. The first-year players included Murray Hall, John Schella, Ed Hoekstra, and Wayne Rutledge, a goalie.

Chicago goalie Andre Gill leaps high to grab puck blasted by Houston's Gordon Labossiere (center) as Ron Anderson (left) of Cougars watches.

(UPI)

Houston goalie Don McLeod pushes puck over to Gordon Labossiere (10) after stopping shot by Chicago's Rosaire Paiement (9) as Aeros' Dunc McCallum gets into play.

Los Angeles Sharks

In their first game the Sharks attracted more people than the Kings of the NHL did in their debut. About 11,000 fans turned up in the Sports Arena, about 2,000 short of capacity. Dennis Murphy, one of the league founders who kept Los Angeles for himself, also acted as the general manager. His coach was Terry Slater. Bart Crashley, Gerry Odrowski and Jim Watson were some of their key players. Early in the season they acquired Alton White from the New York Raiders. White was the only black in big-league hockey, the first to make it since Willie O'Ree played for the Boston Bruins in the 1960's. The Sharks hoped to be able to attract black fans to the game with the addition of White.

Gary Veneruzzo (left) of Sharks and Ted Green of Whalers engage in furious elbowing contest.

(Dan Goshtigian)

New England Whalers

Jack Kelley, who had led the Boston University team to consecutive National Collegiate Athletic Association championships, and was one of the most respected names in college hockey coaching, became the Whalers' coach-general manager. He was luckier than most executives of the new league, in that he had a ready-made market. Before the season began, his club had sold 8,000 season tickets for the Boston Garden and 6,000 seats for the Boston Arena, between which the team would split its games. He also was able to get some of the big names from the NHL—Ted Green, the popular Bruin, Tom Webster, a 30-goal man, and Jim Dorey, Rick Ley, Larry Pleau and Al Smith. In addition, Kelley picked eight players from his Boston University teams. Because of a huge advance sale and the quality of their players, the Whalers were virtually guaranteed success in their first season. They ultimately triumphed in the playoffs against the Winnipeg Jets at season's end, thereby becoming the first championship team in the new league.

Historic First: Larry Pleau (4) scores winning goal in Whalers' opening-game 4–3 victory over Blazers. Bernie Parent is goalie.

(Dan Goshtigian)

Minnesota Fighting Saints

The club started out in the St. Paul Auditorium, a small rink holding 8,000. But midway through the campaign it hoped to move to the new Civic Center, a 16,000-seat arena. The general manager and coach was Glen Sonmor, a former Ranger. Certainly, the area was ripe for hockey. It had supported the Minnesota North Stars of the National League, and before that club was created the area was known as one of the most hockey-conscious centers in the United States. The players included a North Star favorite, Wayne Connelly, along with Jack McCartan, Mike Curran, Ted Hampson, and John Arbour.

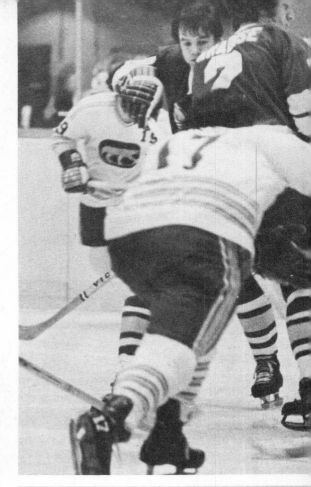

Mike Curran, Saints' goalie, tries to repulse bid by Larry Mavety of Cougars to score, but fails.

(UPI)

Minnesota's Mike Curran blocks attempt by Bob Sicinski to net goal for Chicago.

(UPI)

Billy Klatt of Saints is stymied on shot by Serge Aubry, Quebec goaltender, and J. C. Tremblay of Nordiques clears puck.

(UPI)

New York Raiders

In all major sports, a New York club is essential. The city is the center of television, magazines and newspapers in North America. There was no question of putting a team in New York; the question was where, and who would run it. When the Nassau Coliseum in Long Island wouldn't take the WHA, the rights for the New York franchise of the WHA were sold to Richard Wood, a New Jersey lawyer, and his associates. They began negotiating with Madison Square Garden and the Rangers and finally worked out an agreement to play in the prestigious arena. One NHL owner from another team was angry at this. "It's like inviting a thief into your house for dinner," he said. But the Garden was under a lawsuit alleging antitrust violations, and by renting the building to the new club it avoided charges of conspiring to destroy the league. Wood selected Marvin Milkes, a long-time baseball executive who freely admitted he knew little about hockey, as his general manager. A former and popular Ranger, Camille Henry, was named coach.

The team had several exciting players, including the swift Bobby Sheehan, Ron Ward, Norm Ferguson, and Garry Peters. It was a high-scoring club. Unfortunately, the use of the Garden cost the team more than $20,000 a game and the fans didn't turn out at the beginning as Wood had hoped. The financial burden became too much. Then Milkes left the team and his assistant, Herb Elk, became general manager. Wood asked the league to help him find an owner and James Browitt, the league administrator, took over the running of the club until it could be sold.

Bobby Sheehan of Raiders, after breaking his stick on shot against Sharks' George Gardner, hurries to bench to get another.
(Les Rosner)

Rick Cunningham (left) of Nationals high-sticks Renald Leclerc of Nordiques as Brian Gibbons (6) of Ottawa skates in to aid goalie Les Binkley.

Ottawa Nationals

Ottawa, the capital of Canada, had never been seriously considered for an NHL franchise because the league believed the population was too heavily civil-service and couldn't support a team at high admission prices. Still, Ottawa believed it could. The coach was a former NHL player, Billy Harris, and Buck Houle was the general manager. The team, which included Wayne Carleton, Guy Trotter and Les Binkley, the bespectacled goalie, played in the 9,100-seat Ottawa Civic Center. Its future was unclear. It had money problems from the beginning and the owners were seeking new financing before the club had even played one game.

The rough-and-ready roster of Ottawa Nationals includes (left) Les Binkley, goalie; (center) Rich Sentes, left wing; and (right) Brian Gibbons, defenseman.

Philadelphia Blazers

Derek Sanderson was the big name, of course, and he was joined by his former Bruin teammate, John McKenzie, who was named player-coach at $100,000 a year. In addition, Bernie Parent was in goal, but there weren't any other name players because of the top-heavy salaries paid to the established stars. Most of the squad was composed of Eastern League amateurs. The club couldn't even start its home season on time. The Civic Center, a 9,000-seat arena, was unplayable because the ice didn't freeze. The problem was eventually overcome, but then Sanderson and Parent and McKenzie were injured. The club failed to win its first nine games. Dave Creighton quit as general manager. Phil Watson, a fiery former NHL star, took over the coaching. There were also front-office difficulties and the president of the club, James Cooper, quit over a dispute with Bernie Brown, a millionaire trucker who had put up most of the money. Sanderson was so upset at the way things were going that he offered to return part of his salary.

He didn't have to. The Blazers attempted to get out of the big deal and conferred a $1-million settlement on Sanderson, whereupon he returned to Boston..

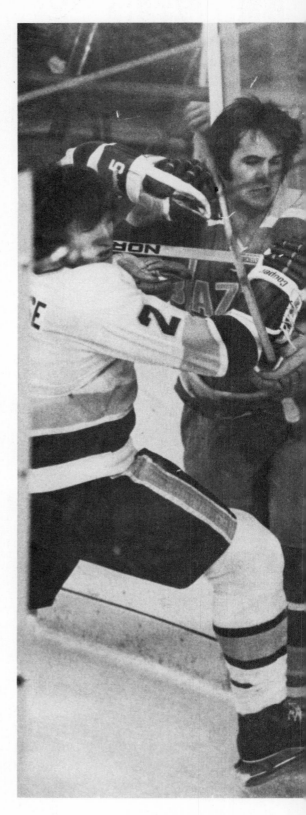

Danny Lawson (right) of Blazers checked against boards by Saints' Dick Paradise.

(UPI)

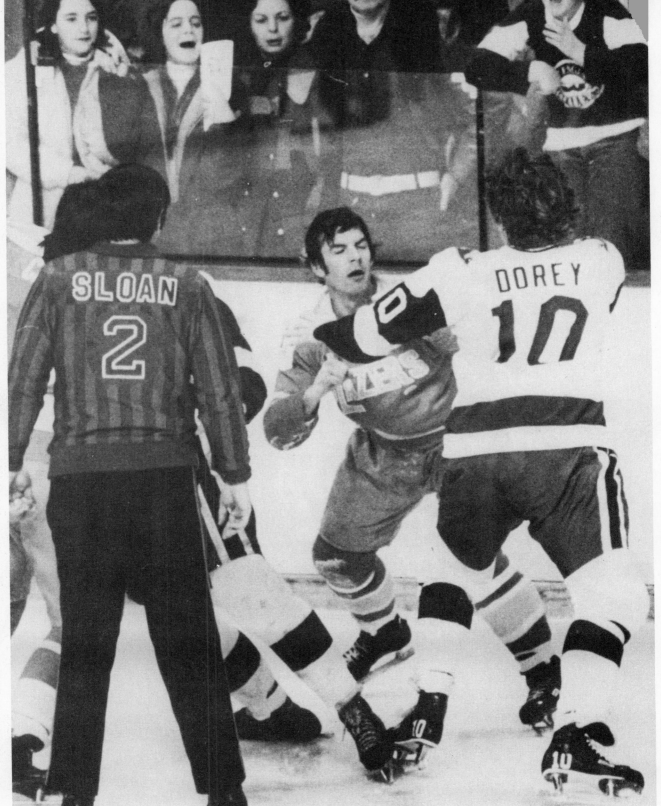

(Dan Goshtigian)

Philadelphia's Jim Cardiff mixes it up with Jim Dorey of Whalers.

Francois Lacombe, Quebec defenseman, upends Terry Caffery of Whalers.

(UPI)

Quebec Nordiques

The Nordiques were a $250,000 purchase from Gary Davidson, president of the league and former owner of the San Francisco franchise. The franchise never fielded a team and was sold to Quebec interests. Hockey fever was high—it always is—in Quebec, but it reached fever pitch when the great Maurice ("Rocket") Richard was named coach of the new club. More than 6,000 season tickets were sold to the 13,000-seat Quebec Coliseum. But Richard quit after only two games because of what he called "the pressure of coaching." He was replaced by Maurice Filion, while Marius Fortier was the general manager. The squad's top player was J. C. Tremblay, who was taken from the Canadiens. It was a French-oriented team with Serge Aubrey in goal and Boom-Boom Caron impressing as a high-scoring minor leaguer.

Quebec's Pierre Guite hustles over, but he's too late to prevent Dunc Rousseau of Winnipeg from chalking up a score.

Winnipeg Jets

The presence of Bobby Hull overshadowed the fact that the Jets had built themselves a solid club. Annis Stukus was the general manager, and although Hull was theoretically the coach, the bench duties were really handled by Nick Mickoski. Besides Hull, there was Bob Woytowich and Christian Bordeleau, and Ernie Wakely and Joe Daley in goal. When owner Ben Hatskin got Hull, he said that about a thousand seats a game in the 8,000-seat Winnipeg Arena would go to pay Hull's salary. Hull was paid, although he couldn't play the early part of the season. But when he finally got into action, he scored three times in five games.

At the end of the season, the team was placed in competition against the New England Whalers for top honors in the new league. Their efforts, though, were not sufficient to overwhelm the Whalers, who became the league's first champions.

Bobby Hull, Winnipeg's star, goes after puck.
(UPI)

Bobby Hull on a sortie toward Chicago goal as Ron Anderson (18) hastens over to try to stop him.
(UPI)